KU-506-960

Contents

Introduction

About this book

This book of revision notes is intended to form a central part of your revision programme. Read this introduction carefully before you attempt to use the notes that follow. It contains some important advice that is intended to help you improve your performance and final grade.

The notes cover all the important subject matter that may be taught as part of the A2 Business Studies course. The content and the examination advice have been fully revised to take into account the changes introduced in 2008. Thus you can use the book with confidence.

The book is divided into two sections to cover Unit 3 and Unit 4 of the AQA A2 Business Studies specification. Each section is divided into chapters that fit precisely with the AQA specification. In turn, each of these chapters is divided into topics that follow the AQA specification exactly. So, by working your way through this book, you can be confident that you have covered the specification.

Make sure you are clear which sections of the book relate to the topics you are studying at any given time, and work through the relevant chapter. This will:
- identify any material that you may not have covered
- reinforce your initial learning
- provide a sound basis for revision prior to the examination(s)

Within the text, important terms are put in **bold** to attract your attention. Finally, the 'Examiner's tips' throughout these notes are special pieces of advice written to help you to understand both the subject and how best to approach it.

The AQA A2 Business Studies course

The structure of the course

The A2 qualification has two units of study:
- **Unit 3: Strategies for success.** This unit commences with a brief introduction to **functional** aims and objectives. Thereafter it looks at the functional strategies that businesses can adopt: marketing, financial, human resource and operations strategies. The study of functional objectives includes understanding the functional objectives that businesses may pursue when drawing up their strategies and also calculating and interpreting relevant data.
- **Unit 4: The business environment and managing change.** In contrast to Unit 3, this unit commences with a brief introduction to **corporate** aims and objectives. Unit 4 takes a strongly evaluative approach to examining the external factors that may act as a catalyst for change, and encourages you to consider these factors in the context of a diverse range of businesses. The final element is entitled 'Managing change' and this considers the importance of factors such as corporate and contingency planning, leadership, culture and the role of project management as part of the process of managing change successfully.

The A2 'story'

There is a story running through the AQA A-level Business Studies specification. Understanding the story will help you to study the subject and to tackle the examinations successfully. You will remember that Unit 1 of the AS course covered the issues involved in planning and financing a business, and took the story to the point at which the business started trading. Unit 2 continued to look at small and medium-sized businesses, and to consider how managers might use functional, tactical decisions to improve the performance of the business.

The story continues with the A2 specification. It is equally important that you understand this element of the story.

Unit 3 is based on large businesses, most of which will be public limited companies. It looks at the strategic decisions that managers can take to improve the performance of the business. These strategic decisions are functional, representing marketing strategies, financial strategies and so on. The businesses will be trading in national and possibly international markets. There is some emphasis on measuring the performance of businesses and this may involve calculations as well as interpreting data. The data will be used to shape future functional strategies.

The story is completed with Unit 4. The first part of Unit 4 assesses the external factors that can promote change in the business environment and the ways in which different types of business may respond. The causes of change include economic, social and political factors. The second element of the unit looks in detail at the ways that businesses can manage change and evaluates the importance of key determinants such as leadership and project management.

The examinations

The Unit 3 examination

This examination is a decision-making case study with a duration of 1 hour and 45 minutes. The case study will include text and a number of appendices of data, setting out a scenario based on a strategic decision that a business has taken or is considering. There will be approximately four questions worth a total of 80 marks. One of the questions is likely to involve a calculation. The final question will be heavily weighted in terms of marks (over 30) and will involve you analysing a particular scenario and making and supporting a recommendation.

An example of a Unit 3 examination can be seen in Chapter 6, pages 76–79.

The Unit 4 examination

The Unit 4 examination is in two parts. The first part relates to a pre-issued research assignment. This assignment will require you to look at a small section of the Unit 4 specification in some detail and will offer precise guidance to direct your research. The examination will comprise a brief piece of text and possibly some supporting data, and two questions of which you choose one. The text and data provide a context for you to apply the findings of your research. The second part of the Unit 4 examination is an essay from a choice of three. Each part of the examination is worth 40 marks, giving 80 in total. The time allowed is 1 hour and 45 minutes.

An example of a Unit 4 examination can be seen in Chapter 10, page 139.

You can find copies of past and specimen AQA A2 Business Studies papers on the AQA website at: **www.aqa.org.uk/qual/gce/business_studies_new.php.**

How to revise for AQA A2 Business Studies

- **Plan well ahead.** This is the most important thing about preparing for examinations in A2 Business Studies.

- **Note down the dates of your examinations.** The AQA GCE Business Studies course has unit examinations: that is, exams on the individual units comprising the qualification. These unit examinations take place in January and June of each year. You will already have taken two examinations at AS, and will take a further two at A2 to complete the A-level Business Studies course. However, you may choose to re-sit one or more of the unit examinations, so the total number of examinations is likely to be more than four.

- **Make sure you know exactly what material you need to revise for the examination and the style of the examination.** Does the exam take the form of a case study, data-response question(s), an essay, or a combination of these? You should plan a full programme of revision well ahead of any examinations you may be taking.

- **Plan your revision carefully.** If you do not like a section of the specification, make sure you revise it early so that you can iron out any problems — perhaps with help from your teacher or lecturer. He or she will also be able to comment on your revision plans.

- **Look at past papers.** You should have a complete set of past papers. They are invaluable for examination practice. They allow you to see topics that have been examined recently and those not tested for some time. They also enable you to familiarise yourself with the style and level of questions that you will encounter on the day of the examination. Past papers should play a greater role in the later stages of your revision programme. You need to have mastered the subject matter before you start practising past questions. It is also helpful to get hold of copies of at least some of the associated marking schemes. These will allow you to see the sorts of answers that examiners were anticipating to each question and the types of examination skills that you were expected to use.

- **Use these Exam Revision Notes as the centrepiece of your revision.** This book will provide you with all the basic information you require. Don't hesitate to write in the book. Tick off subjects as you feel confident about them. Highlight those topics you find difficult and look at them in detail, using your class notes and textbook to support your study.

- **Make sure that you cover all the topics that may form a part of the examination.** Don't skip topics. Plan your revision programme so that you can work steadily through all the topics in the weeks leading up to the examination. Don't be too ambitious as to how much you can do each week. This means you have to start in plenty of time. This is particularly true if you are revising for several A-level examinations in the same sitting.

- **Take any tips on revision techniques from teachers and friends, but do what works for you.** You might find that you remember topics and interrelationships (e.g. the consequences of high gearing) by drawing spider diagrams. On the other hand, you may benefit from completing lots of past papers.

- **Everyone revises differently.** Find out what routine suits you best: alone or with a friend; in the morning or late at night; in short, sharp bursts or in longer revision sessions. Whatever approach you adopt, build in breaks to ensure you remain fresh.

- **Raise any problems or areas of difficulty with your teacher or lecturer.** It is important to eliminate areas of misunderstanding.

- **Attend any revision classes put on by your teacher or lecturer.** Remember, he or she is an expert at preparing people for examinations.

Don'ts

- Don't leave your revision to the last minute.
- Don't avoid revising subjects you dislike or find difficult — in fact, do them first.
- Don't forget that there is a life beyond revision and exams — build leisure and relaxation into your revision programme.
- Don't cram all night before an exam. You would do better to have a night away from revision.

On the day of the examination

- Have a good breakfast.
- Make sure you know where the exam is being held.
- Give yourself plenty of time to get there.
- Take everything you need — extra pens, water, tissues, a watch, Polo mints.
- If you feel anxious, breathe slowly and deeply to help you to relax.

In the examination room

- **Read the instructions at the top of the exam paper and follow them carefully.** A surprising number of students attempt three questions when they have been asked to answer one, for example. Others attempt all the questions, rather than the specified number. Make sure you don't do this.
- **Skim over the paper, identifying the question areas you have revised for.** Spot the questions you can do. Read them carefully.
- **Manage your time carefully.** The examination paper will state the number of marks given for each element of a question. Prior to entering the exam room, you should have worked out how much time you have to answer each part of a question according to the mark allocation — read the examiner's tip below.

Examiner's tip

The best way to manage your time is to calculate the ratio between marks on the paper and the time allocation for the entire paper. This ratio can then be applied throughout the paper, ensuring that you have time to answer all the questions you should.

Example

Your Unit 3 Business Studies examination lasts for 105 minutes and the paper is worth 80 marks. If you assume that you will spend 15 minutes reading the paper, this leaves you 90 minutes to plan and write your answers. You therefore have 90 minutes to answer questions worth 80 marks. This means you can afford to spend 1 minute on a question for each mark allocated to it. In these circumstances, you should spend about 10 minutes on questions worth 8/9 marks and about 35 minutes on a 30/32-mark question.

- **Read through the paper carefully, especially if you have to make a choice of questions.** It is vital that you are clear about what the questions are asking and, if you have to make a choice, that you choose those questions on which you can perform best.

- **Jot down answer plans before you tackle a question.** Only begin writing when you have a clear idea of what the question calls for and your response. Be prepared to amend your answer plan as you develop your answer. Other ideas and information will come to mind as you write; note them in your plan before you forget them.
- **In planning your answers, ensure you know what examination skills are required.** Some questions simply require knowledge; others call for analysis and/or evaluation (see 'Assessment objectives' below). The command word and the mark allocation will tell you what is required.
- **Refer back to the question.** As you write your responses, glance occasionally at the question you are answering. This will help you to write relevantly.
- You may find it reassuring to **attempt your best question first** to settle your nerves. However, do make sure that the questions are not sequential, with the responses to later questions depending on your earlier answers.
- **If you are stuck on a question, go on to the next.** You can always come back to the unfinished one later.
- **Presentation is important.** Set your work out neatly using plenty of paragraphs. A new paragraph is invaluable to indicate a new aspect of the question, or to show that you are using a new examination skill.
- **This also applies to numerical questions.** Set your work out clearly, spacing it out and showing all relevant calculations. Key figures within your answers should be labelled to assist the examiner. In this way, you will receive credit for your work even if you make an arithmetical error.
- **Stay strictly within the time constraints you have calculated.** It is important that you attempt all the questions in order to maximise your marks.
- **Once the examination is over, relax.** Don't brood over any problems in an exam that is completed. It is better to concentrate on the next examination and then to relax when they are all over.
- **Pace yourself during the examination period.** Following a tough examination, a couple of hours spent with friends or watching television will do you more good than a further session of revision.

Examiner's tips

(1) Ask your teacher or lecturer about tips on how to revise, and also about exam skills.

(2) Take short rests during your time of work and revision. If your mind is tired, you will find it difficult to take anything in.

(3) Plan your work: revise at times when you know you will work at your best.

(4) Start your revision early — this will help to avoid stress.

(5) Exercise: you need exercise to work well. Walk, run, play sport — whatever you enjoy most.

(6) Practise past questions to confirm your subject knowledge and develop the appropriate examination skills.

(7) Plan your time carefully in the examination.

(8) Talk to teachers and friends during your revision period – don't shut yourself away completely.

(9) Relax immediately before an examination to avoid being too tired on the day.

(10) Be sensible: if it upsets you to talk to your friends about an exam when it is over, don't do it. In fact, don't even think about the exam you have finished.

Assessment objectives

You may ask: 'what are assessment objectives'? They are skills you require if you are to succeed in A-level Business Studies, or any other A-level examination for that matter. We have already seen that you will need **understanding** of the subject matter as set out in the specification, but this is not sufficient for success at A-level. You must also have examination skills, such as being able to **apply** your knowledge to the scenario, and to write **analytically** and **evaluatively**. One of the most important formulae to learn for A-level is:

A-level success = subject knowledge + examination skills

Assessment objectives, or examination skills, in A-level Business Studies include:
- knowledge and critical understanding
- application of knowledge to unfamiliar situations
- analysis of problems, issues and situations
- evaluation and synopsis

You will see from this list that knowledge of business studies is only one of a number of skills necessary for success. A critical element of your revision will be to develop these skills. While analysis and evaluation are generally regarded as the key to high grades in A-level Business Studies, application is a skill that students find difficulty in mastering. You should try to think about how the theories and concepts that you study relate to different types of business. For example, why might large retailers operate with lower acid test ratios than large manufacturers? It is important to practise these skills through regular attempts at recent past papers.

Good luck with your revision.

Malcolm Surridge

Unit 3
Strategies for success

CHAPTER 1

Functional objectives and strategies

1 *Using objectives and strategies*

What you need to know:
- functional objectives and their relationship with corporate objectives
- the relationship between functional objectives and strategies

1.1 Functional objectives and their relationship with corporate objectives

Corporate objectives

Corporate objectives are the overall goals of the whole business. They vary according to the size and history of the organisation and the personal aims of the business's senior managers.

A business's corporate objectives could include the following:
- growth — to increase the overall scale of the business
- diversification — looking to sell new products in new markets
- to achieve the maximum possible profits in the long term
- developing innovative goods and services

The setting and communication of clear corporate objectives allows senior managers to delegate authority to more junior employees while maintaining the organisation's overall sense of direction.

Figure 1.1 Functional and corporate objectives

Functional objectives

A **functional objective** is a goal that is pursued by particular functions within the business, such as human resources or marketing. It is likely to have a numerical element and a stated timescale. For example, a business might set a financial objective which is a specific profit figure in relation to the capital available to the business. The objective will also set out the timescale within which this financial objective is to be attained.

Once clear corporate objectives have been set, it is possible for the business to set objectives at functional levels. The achievement of their objectives by the various functional areas of the business will contribute to the overall business achieving its corporate objectives. For example, a business that has a corporate objective of growth will require its human resources function to set and achieve objectives to increase the size or productivity (or both) of its workforce, to enable it to increase its supplies of goods or services. At the same time, the finance function may be setting itself goals of increasing the funds available to the business, to allow the objective of growth to be financed properly.

1.2 The relationship between functional objectives and strategies

A **functional objective** is the goal that is pursued by the particular function of the business. A **functional strategy** is the medium- to long-term plan used to achieve the objective.

Figure 1.2 Functional objectives and functional strategies

The functional objective should be set first (and should contribute to the achievement of corporate objectives) and then the strategy should be devised to attain the functional objective.

Earlier we used the example of a business with a corporate strategy of growth, setting a functional objective within the human resources department of developing a larger and more highly skilled workforce. This will require the managers responsible for the human resource function to devise a strategy to fulfil its functional objectives. The key elements of such a plan may include training employees, recruiting new staff and possibly relocating certain staff.

Understanding financial objectives

What you need to know:
- the nature of financial objectives
- the internal and external influences on financial objectives and how they might vary in importance

1.1 The nature of financial objectives

A **financial objective** is a goal or target pursued by the finance department (or function) within an organisation. It is likely that a financial objective will contain a specific numerical element and also a timescale within which it is to be achieved.

There are a number of financial objectives that a business might pursue.

Cash-flow targets

For many businesses, **cash flow** is vital and an essential element of success. Cash flow is the money flowing into and out of a business. Banks require a steady inflow of cash from depositors to enable them to engage in lending activities. The recent crisis surrounding banks in the UK and other countries has, in part, been due to a lack of cash (or liquidity) being available to these organisations. Without cash, banks do not have the necessary funds to avail themselves of possible profitable lending opportunities.

Other businesses may be growing and need regular inflows of cash to finance the purchase of increasing quantities of inputs such as labour and raw materials. Failure to set financial objectives may result in a business facing financial problems when its expenditure or outflow of cash 'runs ahead' of inflows. Such a situation is described as **overtrading**.

Examiner's tip

Link the functional financial objective to the overall corporate objectives of the business and the objectives set by other functions in the business. In the case of cash-flow targets, the marketing function may set itself objectives such as increasing sales, especially cash sales.

Cost minimisation

This financial objective has become better known over recent years due to the publicity given to low-cost airlines and the Easy Group. A financial strategy of cost minimisation entails seeking to reduce to the lowest possible level all the costs of production that a business incurs as part of its trading activities. In the case of the low-cost or budget airlines, this has included minimising labour costs (some require employees to pay for their own uniforms), reducing administrative costs by, for example, using the internet for booking, and using 'out of town and city' airports to reduce landing and take-off fees charged by airport authorities.

Cost minimisation has clear implications for the objectives (and hence strategies) of other functional areas in the business. Clearly, the managers responsible for the other functions should aim to operate with minimal expenditure in order to support the fulfilment of this financial objective. Such a financial objective is likely to support corporate objectives such as profit maximisation and growth.

Return on capital employed targets

The **return on capital employed** (commonly referred to as **ROCE**) is calculated by expressing the net profits made by a business as a percentage of the value of the capital employed in the business. Stakeholders in a business can compare its current ROCE figure with those achieved by other businesses or by the same business in previous years. We consider ROCE more fully on page 16.

A business might set itself a financial target of 20%. This means that its net profits for the financial year will be 20% of the capital employed in the business. This financial objective is very precise and has the advantage of being relatively simple to measure. Achieving such an objective (which is likely to be a higher figure than that achieved in previous years) can require actions to increase net profits as well as to minimise the value of assets used within the business.

As with the other financial objectives, this has considerable implications for other functions. The marketing function may set objectives in terms of market share to improve profitability. At the same time, the operations department may outsource some production to reduce the amount of capital that the business requires to conduct its trading activities.

Shareholders' returns

Shareholders' returns is a term that is difficult to define precisely. Some writers take a short-term view and say that it is the current share price and any associated dividends that are due in the near future. Other writers take a longer-term view of shareholders' returns and define it as a combination of short-term returns (both share prices and dividends) as well as future share prices and dividends. In either case, it puts emphasis on generating profits and increasing the value of the company, as reflected in its share price.

Increasing shareholders' returns requires the support of the other functions in the business. Minimising costs can be an important element of any strategy implemented to increase shareholders' returns, and this could have significant consequences for the operations and human relations functions within the business. Equally, the marketing function may aim to improve the business's product range and to increase added value to support this financial objective.

1.2 The internal and external influences on financial objectives and how they might vary in importance

The financial objectives that are set and pursued by a business will be influenced by a number of factors, both internal and external. The precise importance of these factors will vary according to circumstances.

Internal factors

Internal factors arise within the business. They include:

- **The corporate objectives of the business.** Arguably this is the most important influence on any financial objective that a business may adopt. As we saw earlier, a financial objective must assist the business in achieving its overall corporate objectives. The corporate objectives are set first, followed by functional objectives that are designed to complement them.

- **The nature of the product that is sold.** If a product's demand is sensitive to price (i.e. if it is price elastic), managers may be more likely to implement and pursue a financial objective of cost minimisation. This financial objective may allow price reduction with a positive impact on future sales.
- **The attitudes and aspirations of the business's senior managers.** If the managers of the business hold large numbers of shares, perhaps as part of a share option scheme or as a result of founding the business, increasing the shareholders' value might be an attractive proposition, especially if a long-run view is taken of this financial objective. On the other hand, managers may seek the recognition that accompanies growth. In such circumstances, a financial objective of cost minimisation may be more appropriate.

Examiner's tip

Remember that financial objectives are not set in isolation from the rest of the business. They will be part of the creation of corporate objectives as well as the objectives of the remaining functions within the business. These are part of a complementary package.

External factors

External factors arise outside the business. They include:
- **The actions of the business's competitors.** It is unlikely that a business will ignore the behaviour of its competitors when setting its financial objectives. For example, a business operating in a highly price-competitive market might consider establishing an objective of cost minimisation to allow it more flexibility in pricing decisions.
- **The availability of external finance.** If a business is experiencing difficulty in raising capital, financial objectives are more likely to centre on profits and profitability. Achieving specific returns in terms of profit will assist in reassuring potential shareholders or investors as to the safety of their investments and the level of expected returns.
- **The state of the market.** If the market for the business's products is expanding, it may lead a business's managers to set more expansive financial objectives, such as higher rates of shareholder returns or higher figures for ROCE. In contrast, in a market in which sales figures are stable or declining, financial objectives may be more cautious. Financial objectives such as goals for cost minimisation or cash-flow targets may be deemed more appropriate in these circumstances.

2 *Using financial data to measure and assess performance*

What you need to know:
- the structure and contents of balance sheets
- how to analyse balance sheets
- the structure and contents of income statements and how to analyse them
- how to assess the strengths and weaknesses of financial data in judging performance

2.1 The structure and contents of balance sheets

Since 2005 there have been significant changes to the way in which public companies in the UK present their accounts. A European Union regulation required public companies to prepare financial statements complying with the International Financial Reporting Standards (IFRS) after 1 January 2005. We will use the IFRS approach, although you may notice some differences in the financial terms used compared to those you may have encountered before.

The **balance sheet** is an accounting statement of the firm's assets and liabilities on the last day of an accounting period. It can be seen as a 'snapshot' of the firm's current state of affairs at a given time. It lists the **assets** that the firm owns and sets these against the balancing **liabilities** — the claims of those individuals or organisations that provided the funds to acquire the assets.

Assets

Assets take the form of non-current assets and current assets.

Non-current assets (previously called 'fixed assets') are those assets, such as machinery, equipment and vehicles, that are bought for long-term use (generally more than a year) rather than for resale.

Current assets are items such as inventories (e.g. raw materials) and unsold goods (previously termed 'stock'), receivables (previously called 'debtors'), money in the bank and cash. All of these current assets will be converted into cash by the end of the financial year.

Tangible assets are those which exist physically, such as vehicles. In contrast, **non-tangible assets** do not exist in a physical form. An example of a non-tangible asset is a business's trademark, such as Nike's 'tick'.

Liabilities

A business's assets will automatically be matched by its liabilities.

Shareholders' equity or **total equity** is the funds invested in a company by shareholders in order to acquire the assets that the business needs to trade. In the case of businesses other than companies, this may be called **capital** or **owners' funds**. It is a liability because the business technically 'owes' it to the investors.

Non-current liabilities are moneys employed in the business that have been borrowed from external sources and will be repaid over the 'long term' (a period longer than 1 year). Examples of non-current liabilities are mortgages, bank loans and debentures.

Current liabilities are debts of the business that will be repaid in the 'short term' (less than 1 year). The most common current liabilities are payables (previously known as 'creditors') and bank overdrafts.

All businesses have a variety of assets and liabilities. Table 2.1 overleaf summarises these and provides examples.

The assets owned by a business are financed by its liabilities. If all the assets of the business are listed on one side of the balance sheet and all the liabilities of the business are listed on the other, the two totals should balance. This is usually shown vertically, as in Figure 2.1 on page 9.

Non-current assets	Current assets	Other assets	Shareholders' equity	Non-current liabilities	Current liabilities
The conventional way to list assets begins with the most illiquid first, i.e. the asset which is most difficult to turn into cash without a loss in its value, and ends with the most liquid asset.			All these are classed as liabilities, even capital, as they are all moneys that at some point will need to be repaid, i.e. if the owners sell the business they will want their money back.		
Tangibles **Freehold land** — land over which the owner has absolute rights and doesn't have to pay rent. **Freehold buildings** — as above. **Leasehold land** — a lease is a legal agreement between the owner of a property and another person to the effect that the other person has use of the property for an agreed period of time. **Plant/ machinery/ equipment** — anything from specialised machinery used in manufacture to computers or even furniture. **Vehicles** — all types. *Intangibles* **Goodwill** — the prestige a business enjoys which adds value over and above the value of its physical assets. **Patents/ copyright** — exclusive rights to make or sell a particular invention. **Trademarks** — build up brand loyalty and thus can be ascribed value like goodwill.	**Inventories** — goods made or bought for resale. **Receivables** — clients who have purchased goods but who have not yet paid. **Prepayments** — items for which the business has paid in advance of the date of the balance sheet (e.g. car insurance). **Cash at bank** — moneys held in a bank or other institution's accounts. **Cash in hand** — physical notes and coins held by the business in safes, in tills or as petty cash.	**Stocks and shares** — held in other companies which will provide the organisation with a financial return or dividend. **Loans** — the situation may arise where the organisations lends another business money. This loan is an asset as the organisation making the loan is receiving the benefit of interest payments.	This represents the funds invested into the business through shareholders buying new share issues as well as any subsequent increase in the value of the business through its trading activities.	**Loans** — money borrowed from an outside agency usually carrying a fixed repayment date and interest charge. **Mortgage** — a form of commercial loan secured against a specific property asset. May or may not be a fixed rate of interest. **Debenture** — an alternative to selling shares, a form of fixed repayment and interest loan stock.	**Payables** — suppliers from whom the business has purchased goods, but whom it has not yet paid. **Accruals** — goods and services that have been used and not yet paid for. **Provision for repayment of debts expected to mature** — loans falling due, taxation and dividend payments.

Table 2.1 Assets and liabilities

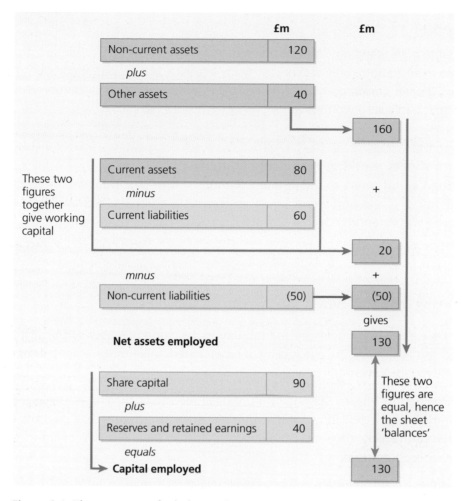

Figure 2.1 The structure of a balance sheet

2.2 How to analyse balance sheets

You should be aware of several aspects of balance sheets when analysing them to make judgements about the financial performance of a business:

- A balance sheet is just a 'snapshot' on one day of the year. If interested parties are examining the accounts several months in the future, the information may be totally out of date.
- The assumption is often made that because a company possesses thousands or millions of pounds' worth of assets, it is doing well. However, the key issue is *how* the company has financed the purchasing of these assets. A business may present a stable position, but the company may face severe problems if it has borrowed heavily and a rise in interest rates occurs.
- External considerations must also be examined, such as the state of the market or economy, the quality of management and skills of the workforce, and the position of similar-sized organisations in the same industry. In the recession, which began in 2008, a 'strong' balance sheet may be one where a business holds a substantial amount of cash and is able to cover its short-term (or current) liabilities, even if sales levels are disappointing.

Balance sheets, working capital and liquidity

Working capital refers to the amount of funds a firm has available for its day-to-day operations. It is the amount of liquid assets that a company has available. **Liquidity** measures the extent to which a business is able to pay its short-term debts.

Working capital is an important measure of a business's liquidity and is given by the formula:

> **working capital = current assets – current liabilities**

Working capital is used to pay for the day-to-day running costs of the firm, such as wages, and to finance the purchasing of replacement inventories. It is also used to fund any sales made on credit terms.

Businesses must ensure that they do not have too many current assets in the form of inventories and receivables (that is, people or organisations that owe the business money). Conversely, they must make sure that they have enough inventories to meet customer requirements.

If a business has too little working capital available, it may struggle to finance its day-to-day operations. Similarly, if it has too much invested in inventories, it may not be able to afford to purchase new fixed assets.

Liquidity is an important concept in business studies and the balance sheets offers an insight into a business's liquidity position. Liquidity measures two factors:

- **The ability of a firm to meet its short-term debts**, as suppliers' bills and expenses can only be met with cash. Liquidity in this sense measures the company's cash or near-cash equivalents as against short-term debts.
- **The ability of a business to turn its assets into cash.** Cash or near-cash equivalents (e.g. bank deposits and receivables) are termed **liquid assets**. Assets that are difficult to turn into cash (e.g. buildings and machinery) are termed **illiquid assets**.

Balance sheets and depreciation

Depreciation is another feature of balance sheets that can be important in analysing the financial performance of the business. Fixed assets have a limited life, even though this could be decades in the case of buildings and some machinery. Instead of charging the full cost of an asset to the year in which it is bought, it is usual to charge some of the cost to each year of the asset's life. This appears as a charge on the profit and loss account and the process is termed 'depreciation'. The term **amortisation** is sometimes used when intangible assets such as goodwill are depreciated.

There are several possible causes of depreciation:
- **Wear and tear.** Through use the asset eventually wears out.
- **Obsolescence.** Eventually a machine will be replaced by faster, more efficient models, though the old machine is still in perfect working order. In some industries, this can occur quickly.
- **Time.** Some assets, such as patents or leases, have a set legal lifetime and therefore lose value as time passes (amortisation).
- **Depletion.** Some natural assets, such as those which are quarried or mined, run out. They can therefore be depreciated in value.

When assets are depreciated each year, the amount of the depreciation is included on the income statement as an expense. This means that the amount of the business's profits may be reduced. Although this may seem like bad news, it is only a 'paper' reduction in profits but has the advantage of reducing the amount of tax that the business has to pay. To avoid this scenario, businesses normally have to work to strict rules imposed by HM Revenue and Customs when calculating deprecation.

Some assets may increase in value rather than decrease. This is called **appreciation**. Normal accounting practice is to ignore this, as it is very subjective. For example, some people may consider that a painting is worth £30 million, while others think it is worthless.

2.3 The structure and contents of income statements and how to analyse them

The structure of income statements

Before the adoption of International Financial Reporting Standards (IFRS) on 1 January 2005, income statements were called **profit and loss accounts**. You may still encounter this term being used in relation to private limited companies and partnerships.

An **income statement** is an accounting statement that shows a firm's sales revenue generated over a trading period and all the relevant costs incurred in earning that revenue (see Figure 2.2 overleaf). **Profit** is the difference that arises when a firm's sales revenue is greater than its total costs. **Loss** is the difference that arises when a firm's sales revenue is less than its total costs.

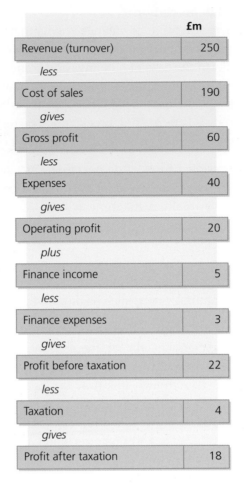

	£m
Revenue (turnover)	250
less	
Cost of sales	190
gives	
Gross profit	60
less	
Expenses	40
gives	
Operating profit	20
plus	
Finance income	5
less	
Finance expenses	3
gives	
Profit before taxation	22
less	
Taxation	4
gives	
Profit after taxation	18

Figure 2.2 The structure of an income statement

Making a profit is one of the most significant business objectives. It is the profit incentive, the reward to be gained, that often motivates people to start out in business in the first place.

In accounting terms, however, the word 'profit' on its own has little actual meaning. Profit is such an integral objective and such a good indicator of company performance that it is broken down into **gross profit** and **operating profit**.

Gross profit

Gross profit is the measure of the difference between sales revenue and the cost of manufacturing or purchasing the products that have been sold.

gross profit = sales revenue – cost of goods sold

Gross profit is calculated without taking into account costs that could be classified as expenses (e.g. administration, advertising) or overheads (e.g. rent, rates).

It is a useful measure. For example, if company A and company B are providing a similar good or service and company A is making a lower level of gross profit than company B, company A must look closely at its trading position. It could, for example, try to find a cheaper supplier.

Operating profit

After calculating gross profit, the next stage is to remove all other expenses and overheads (those costs that are not directly concerned with the trading activities of the business). The result is operating profit.

operating profit = gross profit − (expenses + overheads)

Again, operating profit is a useful measure. A business may find itself making a healthy gross profit but a very small operating profit in comparison to its competitors. This may be because its overheads are not under control. Calculating both gross and operating profit allows owners/managers to identify problem areas with greater ease.

Finance income and finance expenses

Finance income relates to interest that the business receives on accounts that it holds with banks and other financial institutions. **Finance expenses** are the interest that it pays on loans. Financing income and expenses can add to or subtract from a business's operating profit. If its interest received is greater, the difference will be added to operating profit to give a larger figure for profit before taxation. If the interest received is smaller, the net figure will be deducted from operating profit to arrive at profit before taxation.

Profit before and after taxation

All businesses pay tax on their profits. Companies pay corporation tax on profits. At the time of writing, the rate of corporation tax paid by larger companies on profits has just been cut from 30% to 28%. Once tax has been deducted, we arrive at the final figure on the income statement: profit after taxation for the year.

Analysing income statements

In analysing income statements, the following concepts need to be considered:

- **Profit quality.** Profit quality measures whether or not an individual profit source will continue. A company may make one-off profits from the sale of assets, but these may not be a sustainable source of profits and, if so, will be termed 'low-quality profits'. On the other hand, a company with a strong trading position, which can be expected to make profits in future years, is described as generating 'high-quality profits'.

Examiner's tip

This is an important concept to take into account when responding to questions that ask you to consider a company's financial position. Do not just consider the size of the profit figure.

Profit utilisation

Companies may use profit in two main ways:

- **Retained profits.** These are the share of profits kept by the company and added to the company's balance sheet reserves. Retained profits increase the value of the company, so helping an organisation to expand.
- **Distributed profits.** These are the portion of a company's profit shared out to external parties, such as owners or partners, preference shareholders and ordinary shareholders.

A company that retains its profits may perform better in the future.

2.4 How to assess the strengths and weaknesses of financial data in judging performance

There are a number of issues that you may need to consider when assessing the value of financial data in judging the performance of a business.

The importance of comparisons

It is normally very difficult to make a judgement about a business's balance sheet or income statement without having something to compare it with. There are two main possibilities:

- **The performance of the same business in previous years.** It is helpful to compare the profits or net assets employed with the business for the year before and preferably for several years previously. Most company accounts have 2 years' data for each of the key figures and it is normal for the accounts to record a 5-year financial summary. This allows you to consider whether the trend in the data is improving, declining or unchanged.
- **The performance of similar businesses.** It is helpful in making judgements to look at key figures for other, similar-sized businesses and those that operate in the same industries or markets. You can see whether a particular business holds greater levels of inventories, has less or more working capital, or has recorded or retained greater levels of profits over the last trading year.

Judging performance against stated objectives

This gives you a yardstick against which to make and support judgements on the financial performance of a business. If, for example, a business has an objective of growth, it may be reasonable to expect lower profits as it invests more in promotion, research and development, and possibly in reducing prices to increase sales.

Taking into account window dressing of accounts

Window dressing is presenting company accounts in such a manner as to enhance the financial position of the company. It is sometimes termed **creative accounting** and involves making modest adjustments to sales, debtors and stock items when preparing end-of-year financial reports. In many cases, window dressing is simply a matter of making minor changes to the accounts and is not misleading.

Important methods of window dressing are as follows:

- **Massaging profit figures.** Surprisingly, it is possible to 'adjust' a business's cost and revenue figures. Following a poor year's trading, the firm might inflate the revenue earned by the business in the final month of trading by including sales from a later period.
- **Hiding a deteriorating liquidity position.** This allows businesses to improve the look of their balance sheets. For example, a business may carry out a sale-and-leaseback deal just prior to accounts being published — this entails selling a major asset and then leasing it back immediately. This increases the amount of cash in the business and makes it look a more attractive proposition for potential investors.
- **Boosting asset values.** Particularly in the area of intangibles, such as brand valuations and goodwill, companies can state the value of assets as being considerably more than their actual worth.

3   Interpreting published accounts

What you need to know:
● how to conduct ratio analysis
● the value and limitations of ratio analysis

3.1 How to conduct ratio analysis

Ratio analysis is an examination of accounting data through the comparison of two figures. This allows an in-depth interpretation of the data as well as the identification of trends. Ratio analysis measures a number of aspects of a business's performance.

In order to analyse the published accounts of businesses, a well-ordered and structured process has to be followed. The investigation process is shown in Figure 2.3.

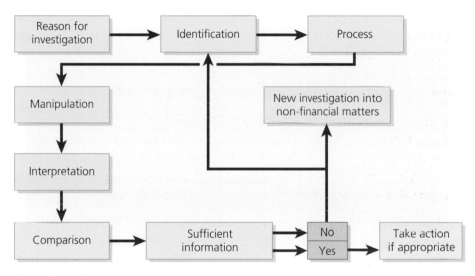

Figure 2.3 The investigation process

Ratios can be classified according to type. They can be used to assess the following aspects of a business's operation:
● profitability
● financial efficiency
● liquidity
● shareholders' ratios
● gearing

Once the reason for the investigation is established, the appropriate range of ratios can be used.

Profitability ratios

Profitability ratios measure the relationship between gross/net profit and sales, assets and capital employed. These are sometimes referred to as **performance ratios**.

Gross profit margin

$$\text{gross profit margin (\%)} = \frac{\text{gross profit}}{\text{turnover (sales)}} \times 100$$

Although higher profit margin results are better, any result must be looked at in the context of the industry in which the firm operates. The level of gross profit margin will vary considerably between different markets. On examination, the firm should be able to make comparisons with previous years' figures to establish whether or not its trading position has become more or less profitable.

Net or operating profit margin

$$\text{net or operating profit margin (\%)} = \frac{\text{net profit}}{\text{turnover (sales)}} \times 100$$

This measure is used to establish whether the firm has been efficient in controlling its expenses. Again, a higher percentage result is better. It should be compared with previous years' results and with other companies in the same industry to judge relative efficiency. The net profit margin should also be compared with the gross profit margin. If the gross profit margin has improved but the net profit margin has declined, profits made on trading are improving. However, the expenses incurred in running the business are increasing at a faster rate than profits. Thus, efficiency is declining.

Return on capital employed (ROCE)

This is sometimes referred to as the 'primary' efficiency ratio and it is considered to be one of the most important ratios. It measures the efficiency of funds invested in the business at generating profits.

$$\text{ROCE (\%)} = \frac{\text{operating profit}}{\text{capital employed}} \times 100$$

As with the other ratios examined so far, a higher value is better, since it can provide owners with a greater return. This figure needs to be compared with those of previous years and other firms to make an informed judgement about the performance of the business. The ROCE for a given organisation also needs to be compared with the percentage return offered by interest-bearing accounts at banks and building societies.

Financial efficiency ratios

Efficiency or activity ratios measure how efficiently an organisation uses its resources. These are sometimes referred to as **asset utilisation ratios**.

Asset turnover

$$\text{asset turnover} = \frac{\text{sales revenue}}{\text{net assets employed}}$$

This ratio measures the efficiency of the use of net assets in generating sales. The figure is normally calculated on an annual basis. An increasing ratio result when compared with previous years indicates increasing efficiency. The business's asset turnover can usefully be compared with those of competitors.

Inventory or stock turnover

$$\text{inventory or stock turnover} = \frac{\text{cost of goods sold}}{\text{average stock held}}$$

This ratio calculates the number of times inventories are sold and replaced. It can only really be interpreted with knowledge of the industry in which the firm operates. For example, if we were examining the accounts of a second-hand car sales business, we might expect it to turn over its entire inventory of cars and replace them with new ones about once a month. Therefore, we would see a result of 12 times. A greengrocer would expect to sell his or her inventories much more frequently.

As usual, we can undertake a comparison with previous years or other similar-sized firms in the same market. As a general rule, a higher rate of inventory turnover (and therefore a higher result) is better. The quicker a business is selling its inventories, the quicker it will realise the profit on it

Debtors' collection period

$$\text{debtors' collection period (days)} = \frac{\text{debtors}}{\text{sales revenue}} \times 365$$

This particular ratio is designed to show how long, on average, it takes the company to collect debts owed by customers. On public companies' balance sheets, customers who are granted credit are called 'trade receivables', but we shall use the term 'debtors' for this ratio. Generally a shorter period is preferable.

Creditors' collection period

$$\text{creditors' collection period (days)} = \frac{\text{creditors}}{\text{sales revenue}} \times 365$$

This particular ratio is designed to show how many days, on average, it takes the company to pay its suppliers. On public companies' balance sheets, people and organisations that are owed money by the business are called 'trade payables' but we shall use the term 'creditors' for this ratio. From a business's point of view, it is best to delay payment, if possible, because it improves the liquidity position.

Examiner's tip

Compare the debtors and creditors' collection periods. If a business takes longer to collect money from debtors (receivables) than it is allowed to pay creditors (payables) then it may encounter problems with its liquidity. Action needs to be taken.

Liquidity ratios

Liquidity ratios investigate the short-term and long-term financial stability of the firm by examining the relationships between assets and liabilities. These are sometimes also called **solvency ratios**.

Current ratio

current ratio = current assets : current liabilities

It is generally accepted that an ideal current ratio is approximately 2:1, i.e. £2 of assets for every £1 of debt or liability. This is because some current assets are inventories, which can be difficult to convert into cash. The acid test ratio overcomes this by excluding inventories.

Acid test ratio

acid test = (current assets – inventories) : current liabilities

Again, conventional wisdom states that an ideal result for this ratio should be approximately 1.1:1, indicating that the organisation has £1.10 to pay every £1 of debt. The company can therefore pay all its debts and has a 10% safety margin as well. A result below this (e.g. 0.8:1) indicates that the firm may have difficulties meeting short-term payments. Some businesses, however, are able to operate with a very low level of liquidity. Supermarkets, for example, can do so because they do not offer customers credit, and income flows into the business immediately a sale is made.

Shareholders' ratios

This group of ratios, also termed **investment ratios**, is concerned with analysing the returns for shareholders. They examine the relationship between the number of shares issued, the dividend paid, the value of shares and company profits.

Dividend per share

$$\text{dividend per share (in pence)} = \frac{\text{total dividends}}{\text{number of issued ordinary shares}}$$

Dividend yield

$$\text{dividend yield (\%)} = \frac{\text{ordinary share dividend (in pence)}}{\text{market price (in pence)}} \times 100$$

Again, a higher result is better. However, the result would once more need to be compared with previous and competitor results.

Gearing ratio

Gearing examines the relationship between internal sources and external sources of finance; it compares the amount of capital raised by selling shares with the amount raised through loans.

Gearing is often included in the classification of liquidity ratios, as it focuses on the long-term financial stability of an organisation. It measures the proportion of capital employed by the business that is provided by long-term lenders, as against the proportion that has been invested by the owners. In this way, we can see how much of an organisation has been financed by debt. It is given by the formula:

$$\text{gearing (\%)} = \frac{\text{non-current assets}}{\text{capital employed}} \times 100$$

The gearing ratio shows the degree of risk involved in investing in a company. If borrowed funds comprise more than 50% of capital employed, the company is considered to be highly geared. Such a company has to pay interest on its borrowing before it can pay dividends to shareholders or reinvest profits. Companies with lower gearing (those below 50%) offer a lower-risk investment and should find it easier to borrow extra funds if necessary.

3.2 The value and limitations of ratio analysis

Ratio analysis is a helpful tool in analysing the published accounts of businesses. Rather than considering a single figure, such as operating profits, ratios give you something to compare the figure against, such as the value of capital available to the business. This allows you to make more informed judgements about performance.

Ratios also look at the vital aspects of a business's financial performance. Thus they consider not just the business's profitability, but also its liquidity, whether it has borrowed too much and whether it is efficient.

Ratios help all of a business's stakeholders – managers, shareholders, creditors, suppliers and customers – to make judgements. The financial performance of a business can be assessed from these perspectives using ratio analysis.

Although ratio analysis is a powerful tool, it does have several drawbacks:
- It is retrospective — ratio analysis concentrates on past performance and is not forward looking. Changes in factors such as the external environment mean that the results of analysing a firm's history may not prove to be a good guide to future performance.
- Different companies may use different accounting policies, making true comparison difficult.
- Ratio analysis provides no information about non-financial matters, such as the state of the market, the morale of the workforce and the experience of management.
- Ratio analysis does not take into account the effect that inflation may have on reported figures, especially sales.
- It is difficult to compare like with like, as companies are rarely the same in terms of size, product mix and objectives.

4 *Selecting financial strategies*

What you need to know:
- the range of financial strategies available to a business

4.1 The range of financial strategies available to a business

A **financial strategy** is a medium- to long-term plan designed to achieve the objectives of the finance function or department of a business.

Raising finance

A business has to consider how it will raise the capital it needs to purchase non-current assets, pay for research and development, buy other companies or implement new marketing plans. There are two major approaches to raising finance:

- **Borrowing.** Some managers may elect to raise substantial sums through borrowing from banks or other financial institutions. This has the advantage of being relatively quick to arrange, especially if the business has non-current assets that can be used as **collateral** against the loan. (Collateral is security for the creditor — it can be sold to repay the loan if the business defaults on its payments.) This strategy for raising finance commits the business to regular interest payments, which may mean that it is less attractive to a business that is not profitable or one that has experienced cash-flow problems.
- **Selling shares.** An alternative approach is to sell shares in the business. This is slower and can be relatively expensive. It can also be a difficult proposition at certain times if the business's share price is declining. It may also dilute the control that a particular group of shareholders holds in the organisation. However, it does offer substantial advantages to the business. It does not commit the business to regular interest payments, irrespective of its financial position. Instead the managers will be expected to pay a share of the company's profits to the shareholders (this payment is known as **dividends**). Clearly, if the company is experiencing a period of low profits, it always has the option to reduce the amount it pays in dividends.
- **Other sources of finance.** Some businesses may be in the fortunate position of holding non-current assets or holdings in other companies that can be sold to raise funds for investment in the business. This is an ideal means of raising finance in that it avoids any sort of payment. However, for many businesses this will not be an option.

Implementing profit centres

A **profit centre** is an area, department, division or branch of an organisation that is allowed to control itself separately from the larger organisation. It makes its own decisions, following corporate objectives, and may produce its own income statement for amalgamation with the rest of the business. This might be an attractive financial strategy for a number of reasons, both financial and non-financial:

- Allocating costs and profits on a specific area basis allows for more accurate decision making. Businesses can assess how relatively small sections of the organisation are performing and therefore take more informed decisions.
- Monitoring of budgets, targets and performance is much easier with smaller areas.
- Decentralised decision making allows areas to make decisions faster and to be more responsive to changes in local conditions.
- Delegated power and authority improves motivation.
- It is easier to generate a good teams-working spirit in smaller, more autonomous groups.

A wide range of businesses use profit centres. British Airways operates most of its routes as separate profit centres and Starbucks' coffee shops are organised as separate profit centres.

Examiner's tip

Consider the value of profit centres in relation to the type of business concerned. They may be attractive to a business that operates a large number of discrete sections or branches.

However, there are a number of disadvantages from using of profit centres:
- Profit centre allocation can cause rivalry between centres, with centres competing among each other rather than with other businesses.
- Individual centres can become too narrowly focused and lose sight of overall business objectives.
- Communication between centres can become difficult and slow.
- Coordinating the activities of many small areas is complex.
- Performance of individual areas may be adversely or favourably affected by local conditions, making it difficult to analyse and compare.
- The allocation of costs can be complicated, expensive and inaccurate. Costs can act as a de-motivator if managers do not take ownership of them because they feel the costs have been imposed.
- The business is likely to have to invest heavily in training to provide staff with the skills necessary to manage more autonomously.

Cost minimisation

This can be classified as a financial strategy as well as a financial objective. Businesses will seek to implement a cost minimisation strategy by implementing a number of possible policies:
- **Minimising labour costs.** This may be important for firms supplying services, as many of them are likely to face wage and salary expenses that are a high proportion of total costs. Therefore cutting labour costs can have a substantial impact on overall costs of production.
- **Relocating.** Moving to eastern Europe or Asia will assist in reducing labour costs and also overheads such as building costs. However, in the case of manufacturing the cost advantages may be offset to some extent by increased transport costs. Relocating has been a popular approach with businesses that supply financial services such as banking and insurance.
- **Using technology.** Technology can replace expensive staff for businesses located in high labour cost countries such as the UK. Thus, the low-cost airlines rely heavily on the internet to process bookings for flights and to facilitate a speedy and inexpensive check-in procedure for passengers.

Cost minimisation has significant implications for the other functional areas of the business. For example, the marketing department will have to develop a marketing strategy based on a low-cost, low-price product. Similarly, it may have profound implications for the business's operational strategy if, for example, a fair proportion of the business's production takes place overseas.

Allocating capital expenditure

Capital expenditure is spending on new non-current assets such as property, machinery and vehicles. The way in which a business decides to spend its capital can have a significant effect on the operation of its finance department, and also impact on the other functions in the business. Businesses only have access to a limited amount of capital and any expenditure decisions normally have significant opportunity costs.
- **Investing in machinery.** Businesses may opt to do this to reduce the amount of labour deployed in the organisation and the associated costs. This approach will involve heavy initial expenditure on capital items but may lead to a reduction in expenditure at a later stage. It also offers the potential advantage of increasing the productivity of the business. Nissan's car manufacturing plant in Sunderland has one

of the highest levels of labour productivity in Europe. In part this is due to the extensive use of technology on the production line. There are drawbacks, however. The initial costs are high and workers may need retraining in order to operate the technology efficiently.

- **Investing in property.** Some businesses invest heavily in property to enable them to trade effectively or possibly to support their corporate image. For example, supermarkets in the UK hold a portfolio of property in high street and out-of-town locations which is essential to enable them to conduct their business effectively. Some also hold considerable amounts of land for possible development as sites, but also to prevent competitors from acquiring it. Hotels and restaurants may purchase desirable property in prosperous locations to support an upmarket corporate image. In both cases, allocating capital expenditure in this way can help the business to attain its overall corporate objectives.

5 Making investment decisions

What you need to know:
- how to conduct investment decisions
- the criteria used in making investment decisions
- the ways in which risk and uncertainties in investment decisions are assessed
- the quantitative and qualitative influences on investment decisions

5.1 How to conduct investment decisions

In business studies, investment has two main meanings:
- buying part or all of another business
- buying a certain fixed asset

Investment decisions involve risk — resources are to be risked in a venture that may (or may not) bring rewards.

In this section, we are concerned with whether or not to purchase a non-current or fixed asset. We will further assume that the business is profit maximising — it will choose the item of equipment that provides the highest return on the initial investment rather than one that is more environmentally friendly.

There are two major considerations when deciding whether or not to invest in a fixed asset:
- the total profits earned by the fixed assets over the asset's useful life
- how quickly the asset will pay off its cost

The process of assessing these factors is called **investment appraisal**. There are three main methods of investment appraisal:
- payback
- average rate of return
- net present value

Payback
Payback simply means the number of years it takes to recover the cost of an investment from its earnings.

Example

A machine is bought for £10,000. The purchaser makes an estimate of the additional revenue for each year that will be generated as a result of using the machine, and the annual direct and maintenance costs required to support this revenue.

	£
Sales	20,000
Less:	
Wages	5,000
Materials	6,000
Overheads	700
Maintenance	300
Extra income	8,000

If the machine cost £10,000, the investment will pay for itself in 1.25 years. This is found by using the formula:

payback = number of full years + (amount of cost left/revenue generated in next year)

additional revenue generated in 1 year = £8,000, so amount left to pay = £2,000; revenue generated in next year = £8,000.

So payback = 1 + (2,000/8,000) = 1.25 years.

This technique is quick and simple but ignores the timing of payments and receipts.

Average rate of return

This calculates the percentage rate of return on each asset as follows:

$$\text{average rate of return} = \frac{\text{average annual profit}}{\text{asset's initial cost}} \times 100$$

where:

$$\text{average profit} = \frac{\text{total net profit before tax over the asset's lifetime}}{\text{useful life of asset}}$$

Example

Machine A will make a profit of £200,000 over 5 years and cost £100,000.

total profit over 5 years	=	£200,000
average annual profit	=	£200,000/5
	=	£40,000
average rate of return	=	$\frac{£40,000}{£100,000} \times 100 = 40\%$

The average rate of return is considered to be more useful than payback because it pays attention to varying cash flows. The final figure should be compared with the rate of interest or alternative investments.

Net present value

The average rate of return method fails to take into account that cash in the hand now is worth more than cash received in the future. Payback ignores profitability. However, the **net present value** (NPV) approach takes into account profits *and* the timings of payments and receipts.

Discounted cash flow converts future earnings from an investment into their present values. These present values are then added up and the cost of the investment subtracted from the total. What remains (if anything) is the net present value (NPV). NPV must be positive for the investment to be worthwhile.

Example

An investor deposits £1,000 in a savings account. In return, the bank pays a rate of interest. If the rate of interest is 10%, at the end of 1 year the investment will be worth £1,100.

After 2 years: (£1,100 + 10%) = £1,210

And after 3 years: (£1,210 + 10%) = £1,331

At the end of 3 years, the investor has £1,331 that was only worth £1,000 3 years ago. Looked at in another way, the current or present value of £1,331 in 3 years' time is £1,000. This is because (assuming an interest rate of 10%) the £1,000 can be invested now to be worth £1,331 in 3 years.

To save us having to perform endless repetitive calculations that have been done time and time before, discounted cash flow tables are available which relate rates of interest to a period of time in years.

Example

An investment project costs £6,000. The rate of interest is 10% and the project will yield returns for 5 years of £1,800 per year.

Year	Cash flow		Discounting factors (from table)		Present value
0	6,000	×	1.00	=	(6,000)
1	1,800	×	0.909	=	1,636.20
2	1,800	×	0.826	=	1,486.80
3	1,800	×	0.751	=	1,351.80
4	1,800	×	0.683	=	1,229.40
5	1,800	×	0.621	=	1,117.80
			Net present value	=	£822.00

If the resulting figure is positive, the investment project is worthwhile. If the result is negative, the project should not be undertaken. A high figure is preferred to a lower one.

5.2 The criteria used in making investment decisions

Once the investment appraisal process has produced an answer, this needs to be compared with something in order to make a decision. There are a number of criteria that a business may use to make an investment decision:

- **The rate of interest.** Average rate of return and net present value produce figures that can be compared with the rate of interest. Any interest rate chosen for this process will be based on the interest rate set by the Bank of England (see pages 99–100). In essence, the managers of the business will seek a return that is greater than the current and forecast interest rates, if the average rate of return is used. In the event of using NPV, the current interest rate should produce a positive net present value.
- **Other possible investments.** It is perhaps unusual for a business to consider only a single investment proposal. Investment appraisal techniques may be used to compare several competing investments, from which the business may only select one. Thus **opportunity cost** is an important influence here.

5.3 The ways in which risk and uncertainties in investment decisions are assessed

Risk is the chance of something adverse or bad happening. It is not a simple matter to assess the degree of risk involved in an investment decision. In the context of investment decisions there are two broad possibilities: costs may be higher than forecast or sales lower than expected.

Forecasting future sales can be a difficult, and often expensive, exercise. Market research can be used, but it is costly and not always reliable. Equally, costs may rise above the forecast level. In 2008, the price of oil and many other materials used in manufacturing rose unexpectedly. In many cases, companies attempt to take decisions about investment projects based on inaccurate data.

Managers may seek to identify and manage the risk in investment decisions by purchasing raw materials on forward markets (i.e. setting the price now for future delivery), by building in allowances for fluctuations in sales revenue and costs, and by ensuring the business has sufficient financial assets to deal with any adverse circumstances.

5.4 The qualitative influences on investment decisions

As part of their investment decisions, organisations consider other factors, such as the possible effects on industrial relations, the likely reactions of competitors and the impact of the decision on the business's corporate image. Today many businesses that are investing in major projects have to consider the environmental consequences of their decisions. To be seen not to consider such a high-profile factor may constitute an own goal in terms of public relations.

CHAPTER 3 Marketing strategies

1 Understanding marketing objectives

What you need to know:
- the nature of marketing objectives
- the internal and external influences on marketing objectives

Strategy is the medium- to long-term plan required to achieve a business's overall objectives. The **marketing strategy** is the contribution made by the marketing department to this process. Developing a marketing strategy requires:
- careful analysis of the firm's current position
- complete understanding of the business and the market in which it operates
- some assessment of the resources available to the business

1.1 The nature of marketing objectives

Marketing strategy entails the setting of **marketing objectives**. Marketing objectives are medium- to long-term targets that may provide a sense of direction to the marketing department and to the whole business. This is especially true if the targets are quantified. A business might set a range of marketing objectives, including the following:
- **To increase or maintain market share.** For example, a company might seek to increase market share (as measured by value of sales) from 20% to 25% over the next 3 years. Alternatively, it may decide to introduce a new product to maintain its current market share. For example, Mercedes introduced a small car to protect itself from increasing competition in the luxury car market.
- **To broaden its range of products to improve its market standing.** A company may adopt an asset-led approach by using an existing brand name to develop new products. The Virgin Group is a classic example of this approach.
- **To break into a new market (or market segment).** Kellogg's, for example, has marketed its breakfast cereals as a product that can be eaten at any time of the day.

1.2 The internal and external influences on marketing objectives

The precise marketing objectives a firm might set will depend on a variety of factors, the relative importance of which will vary from business to business.

Internal factors
- **The business's corporate objectives.** These are clearly a major determinant, since the achievement of the business's marketing objectives should assist it in achieving its corporate objectives. Therefore the two sets of objectives should be interrelated.
- **The size and type of firm.** Large firms possessing high degrees of market power may set more expansive and aggressive marketing objectives. In contrast, new entrants to a market or smaller businesses may be less ambitious in the scope of such objectives.
- **The financial position of the business.** A business that is profitable or has a strong cash-flow position may be able to engage in the necessary research and development of marketing campaigns to set marketing objectives that are challenging.
- **The possession of a USP.** A business that has a unique selling point (or proposition) may set objectives reflecting an expectation of substantial increases in market share or brand recognition. Having a feature that differentiates the business or its products allows this to be a more realistic objective.

External factors

- **The business's position in the market.** A dominant business may be able to break into new market segments and build on its existing brand image. Kellogg's (as described above) provides an example of such an approach.
- **The expected responses of competitors.** Whether rivals might match any actions taken to achieve particular marketing objectives can be a major determinant in the objectives that are set. This might be particularly influential when the businesses concerned are of similar size and financial power.
- **The state of the economy.** If the economy is growing slowly or not growing at all (as may be the case in many countries in 2009), marketing objectives will be more conservative, especially for businesses that sell luxury items. Conversely, in a period of economic boom, the opposite may be true.

Examiner's tip

This is a topic on which you could be required to write evaluatively. The marketing objectives set by a business depend upon the type of factors listed above. The key point is that we cannot say with certainty what objectives a firm might set. We need to consider the circumstances of the business and the environment in which it operates.

2 Analysing markets and marketing

What you need to know:
- reasons for, and the value of, market analysis
- methods of analysing trends
- the ways in which IT can be used in analysing markets
- difficulties in analysing marketing data

2.1 Reasons for, and the value of, market analysis

Businesses take major marketing decisions regularly. Such decisions are essential and must be successful if a business is to achieve its marketing objectives. Businesses can take two broad approaches to decision making:

- **Decisions based on hunches or instinct.** It is possible for managers to take major marketing decisions, such as whether to introduce a new product, based entirely on instinct. This means that they conduct little or no research and rely on their knowledge of the market.
- **Scientific marketing decisions.** Many factors influence the markets in which businesses trade. Actions of competitors, consumers, suppliers and governments can all have an impact, as can changes in tastes and fashions. It is important to gather as much evidence as possible and to consider it carefully before taking major marketing decisions. This is why analysing the market can be so important.

Hunch or instinct might be a valid approach in a market that regularly experiences rapid change, where market research cannot be used effectively. It may also be that in some fashion markets, decisions taken by businesses on the design and format of products can help to shape consumers' tastes.

However, dependence on guesswork is a risky approach because it is entirely possible to be wrong. For example, incorrectly predicting a surge in demand for a product can result in a business having an embarrassing surplus of products, with a consequent adverse impact on its cash-flow position. It can be argued that the analysis of a market is an expensive exercise, but it might be less expensive than making a major error in forecasting consumer demand.

2.2 Methods of analysing trends

The analysis of marketing data enables firms to:
- forecast future sales, allowing them to produce sufficient quantities of a product to avoid the accumulation of surplus stocks or unfulfilled orders
- assess consumer reactions to the products they are selling
- estimate the future need for resources such as labour, allowing recruitment or redeployment in advance of changes in demand

Central tendency and normal distributions

Firms may need to reorganise data into a form that can be used by decision-makers in the business. It may, for example, be necessary to identify the most common figure from a range of data. This single figure can be used to represent the entire group of data. Such figures are referred to as **measures of central tendency**. There are three principal measures of the central tendency of data:
- **Arithmetic mean** — commonly referred to as the 'average'. This is calculated by adding the value of all items in the data and then dividing this total by the number of items.
- **Median** — the middle number of a range of data when the figures are placed in ascending or descending order.
- **Mode** — the most common number among a set of data. In other words, the mode is the value that occurs most frequently.

The **normal distribution** of data is a frequency distribution possessing a symmetrical pattern, as shown in Figure 3.1 overleaf. Normal distributions tend to occur when data are collected frequently. Data exhibiting a normal distribution have the following characteristics:
- Within a normal distribution, mode = mean = median.
- The number of results above the average will be exactly equal to the number of results below it.

The normal distribution is useful in statistical quality control. It can provide data by which components and other items subject to variation can be assessed — and rejected if necessary.

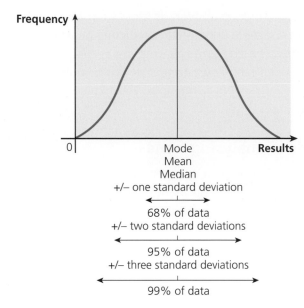

Figure 3.1 *A normal distribution*

Analysing trends: extrapolation

A **trend** is an underlying pattern of growth or decline in a series of data. By establishing whether sales trends, for example, are rising or declining, a firm can plan production to meet the demands of the market as fully as possible.

Managers are very interested in future trends in the markets in which they trade. Having an insight into future trends can assist firms in taking correct marketing decisions. **Extrapolation** is a relatively simple technique that can assist forecasting.

Extrapolation analyses the past performance of a variable such as sales and extends this into the future. If a firm has enjoyed a steady increase in sales over a number of years, the process of extrapolation is likely to forecast a continued steady rise.

Extrapolation can assist managers in identifying market segments that are likely to experience growth or decline, so they can plan production accordingly. Extrapolation simply extends the apparent trend by eye, as shown in Figure 3.2.

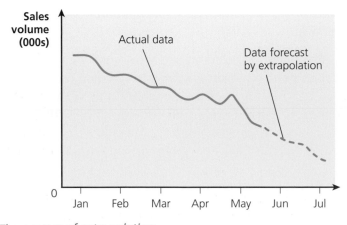

Figure 3.2 *The process of extrapolation*

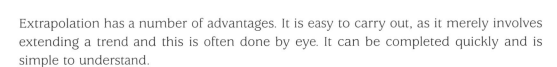

Extrapolation has a number of advantages. It is easy to carry out, as it merely involves extending a trend and this is often done by eye. It can be completed quickly and is simple to understand.

However, it may be inaccurate because it assumes that the future will be similar to the past. For this reason, it is not suitable for use in environments subject to rapid change. Predicting that sales of a fashion good, such as clothing, will continue to rise on the basis of extrapolation may be unwise, as a change in fashion may provoke a slump in sales.

Analysing trends: correlation

When analysing market trends, firms will attempt to identify whether there is any **correlation** between different variables and the level of sales. Correlation is a statistical technique used to establish the extent of a relationship between two variables, such as the level of sales and advertising.

Correlation can be illustrated by plotting the two variables against each other on a graph. Figure 3.3(a) plots monthly sales figures against the level of advertising expenditure for the same month. Each month's relationship is shown by an X. It is apparent that higher levels of advertising expenditure lead to higher sales. Managers may be encouraged by this result to increase spending on advertising.

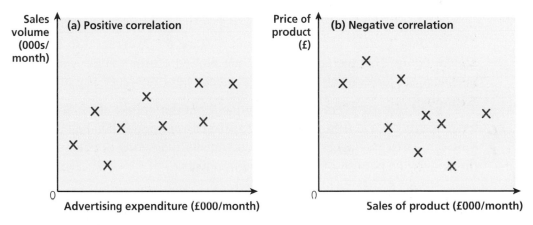

Figure 3.3 *Correlation*

Figure 3.3(b) shows a negative correlation between the price of a product and its sales. From this managers might decide that demand is price elastic and attempt to reduce the price as far as possible.

Correlation only shows a *possible* relationship between two variables. Sales might rise at the same time as a firm increases its expenditure on advertising. However, the two events might not be related. The rise in sales may be due to a competitor increasing prices or the fact that the firm's products have become fashionable. So the results of correlation should be treated with caution.

However, correlation can help to identify key factors that influence the level of sales achieved by a business. For example, there may be a strong positive correlation between sales and income levels. In these circumstances, the business should target markets in which consumers are enjoying rising income levels.

Analysing trends: moving averages

Moving averages are a series of calculations designed to show the underlying trend in a series of data. They can be calculated over various periods of time, although a 3-year moving average, as shown in Table 3.1, is one of the most straightforward to calculate.

Year	Bicycle sales	Three-year moving average
1999	1,500	–
2000	1,550	4,550 ÷ 3 = 1,517
2001	1,500	4,700 ÷ 3 = 1,567
2002	1,650	4,725 ÷ 3 = 1,575
2003	1,575	4,820 ÷ 3 = 1,607
2004	1,595	4,870 ÷ 3 = 1,623
2005	1,700	5,100 ÷ 3 = 1,700
2006	1,805	5,270 ÷ 3 = 1,757
2007	1,765	5,470 ÷ 3 = 1,823
2008	1,900	5,545 ÷ 3 = 1,848
2009	1,880	–

Table 3.1 Annual sales of George Ltd, bicycle manufacturers

In this example the 3-year moving average is calculated by gradually moving down the data, adding 3 years' sales together and dividing the result by 3 to obtain an average annual figure. The average figure is then plotted on the middle year of the three in question. So, for example, the moving average for 1999–2001 is plotted next to 2000.

The use of moving averages should smooth out the impact of random variations and longer-term cyclical factors, including seasonal variations, thus highlighting the trend. This can assist managers in taking good-quality marketing decisions, as they can see the underlying pattern of sales for their products.

2.3 The ways in which IT can be used in analysing markets

Information technology (IT) has a range of uses in collecting and analysing marketing data.

Collecting marketing data

It is possible for businesses to use IT as a means of collecting market research data. For example, you might be persuaded to fill in an online survey in return for being entered into a prize draw. IT can collect data on people's spending habits in a variety of ways. Online spending is simple for firms to record and analyse. This can reveal spending patterns of which managers can take advantage. For example, it may show that certain groups of products are purchased together. As a result, the business concerned may market these products together. The online retailer Amazon records its customers' purchases and promotes similar products to them at a later date.

A number of supermarkets and other retailers use loyalty cards. One purpose of these cards is to encourage customer loyalty and therefore repeat purchases. However, they also enable the business to collect data on customers' purchases and to relate them to personal data they have on these customers. Thus, they are able to analyse electronically the types of people who purchase particular products, allowing for better-focused advertising campaigns.

Analysing marketing data

Data that are collected electronically can be analysed and presented using IT. This is a relatively cheap method of data analysis and also a highly flexible one. Data can be analysed in a variety of ways and presented in different formats to ensure that all the messages they contain are understood.

It is possible to argue that in many cases the speed of data analysis afforded by IT may be more of an advantage than its relatively low cost.

2.4 Difficulties in analysing marketing data

Marketing data can give the wrong message for a number of reasons:
- The samples on which the forecasts are based may be too small. This could mean that the views expressed by those in the sample are not representative of the entire population of potential consumers.
- Some industries are subject to rapid change. Examples are mobile telephone and other high-technology industries. Delays between gathering the data and presenting the results to those who take marketing decisions may mean that the market has changed.
- Major changes in the external environment can have substantial effects on the decisions of purchasers. A rise in interest rates, for example, may lead to many consumers delaying or abandoning their decision to purchase, especially if the product in question is bought on credit. Similarly, the introduction of a new competitor into the market could cause sales to plummet.

3 *Selecting marketing strategies*

What you need to know:
- the major marketing strategies that can be used
- how to assess the effectiveness of marketing strategies

3.1 The major marketing strategies that can be used

Low cost versus differentiation

One way of thinking about marketing strategies is to consider businesses that base their strategy on being low cost. We have already discussed low-cost financial strategies on page 21. They offer businesses a way of attracting customers and can be used by businesses that are late entrants to a market and do not have an established brand name or customer base. They can be highly effective if demand for the product is price elastic. Airlines such as easyJet have used this marketing strategy to great effect and have captured market share from established airlines, particularly British Airways. However, it does require the business to have a low cost base and to be able to maintain or reduce its cost levels as established suppliers begin to respond to the challenge.

An alternative approach is to opt for differentiation. This means that a business makes its product distinctive from those of its rivals and gives consumers a reason to purchase it and to become brand loyal. The Co-operative Bank presents itself as ethical and environmental and, using this strategy, has competed successfully against much larger financial organisations.

Ansoff's matrix

A major way to assess a variety of marketing strategies is to use **Ansoff's product–market matrix**, illustrated in Figure 3.4. It assists businesses in evaluating the organisation and the market in which it operates. Developed by Igor Ansoff in 1957, it represents a useful framework for considering the relationship between marketing and overall strategy.

The matrix considers product and market growth and analyses the degree of risk attached to the range of options open to the business. The key findings of Ansoff's matrix are:

- Staying with what you know (e.g. market penetration) represents relatively little risk.
- Moving into new markets with new products is a high-risk strategy.
- Assessment is made of the value of each option.

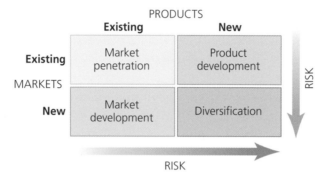

Figure 3.4 Ansoff's matrix

We can look at Ansoff's matrix in more detail.

Market penetration

In this situation, the business's strategy is to market existing products to its existing customers more strongly. By making this choice the business avoids the commitment in terms of expense and time of developing new products or investigating and analysing unfamiliar markets. In this way, the strategy can be implemented relatively quickly and cheaply.

However, it may be that the market is saturated (few, if any, new customers exist), and therefore the only way to increase sales is by taking customers away from competitors. This is the situation that mobile phone service providers such as Vodafone are experiencing. A policy of market penetration in these circumstances can necessitate heavy expenditure on promotion and some flexibility in pricing decisions. Because this marketing strategy does not involve new products or new markets, it is categorised as low risk.

Market development

This strategy involves a business targeting its existing product range at potential customers in a new market. This means that the product remains the same, but it is marketed to a new audience. New markets could be overseas or possibly a different segment within a domestic market. Well-known companies such as McDonald's and Starbucks have engaged in a strategy of market development as they have introduced their products to countries across the globe. One way to achieve market development is through a joint venture with an existing supplier. Tesco has used this approach in China.

This strategy is classified as medium risk because the product or products are unchanged and presumably the business's managers are familiar with their strengths and weaknesses. It also avoids the need for developing new products, which can be costly and time consuming. However, it has drawbacks in that the products may not be accepted in the new markets or they might need expensive modifications if they are to sell in profitable numbers. McDonald's has encountered some resistance to its expansion, most notably in India and France.

Product development

This strategy requires that a new product be marketed to a business's existing customers. The business develops and innovates new product offerings to replace or supplement existing ones. Tesco has engaged in product development (as well as market development) by selling electrical products and financial services to its existing grocery customers.

The advantages of this approach are that the business knows its customers and is in contact with them already, making it easier to conduct market research and promote any new products. The business may also have a strong brand name that it can attach to its new products. Product development has been a key strategy of the Virgin Group. The downside of this strategy is that the business may engage in producing and selling products in which it has limited expertise and it may be vulnerable to the actions of more established businesses in the market. The balance of advantages and disadvantages means that this strategy is categorised by Ansoff as medium risk.

Examiner's tip

It is vital that you consider the risks and benefits of these strategies in relation to national and international markets. Consider also how businesses might actually implement such strategies.

Diversification

This is where a business's marketing strategy is to sell completely new products to new customers. There are two types of diversification: related and unrelated diversification. **Related diversification** means that a business remains in a market or industry with which it is familiar. An example of this is Virgin moving into rail transport when it already operated Virgin Airlines. **Unrelated diversification** is where the business has no previous industry or market experience. This took place when Virgin began to produce vodka.

This is a high-risk strategy, as the business lacks experience of the product and the customer base that it is targeting. As a consequence, it will have greater need of market analysis to guide its marketing decisions and more chance of taking the wrong decisions.

3.2 How to assess the effectiveness of marketing strategies

The ultimate means of assessing the effectiveness of a particular marketing strategy is to compare it to the marketing objectives that were set prior to the implementation of the strategy. If these are fulfilled, the strategy can be deemed to have been successful. A further key means of judgement is to assess the extent to which the marketing strategy has enabled the business to achieve its corporate objectives.

Other measures can also be applied. It may be that a successful marketing strategy will result in other businesses copying it. The first low-cost airline was South West Airlines in the USA. It is a tribute to the success of its low-cost strategy that it has been copied in markets across the world.

4 Developing and implementing marketing plans

What you need to know:
- the major components of marketing plans
- the major internal and external influences on marketing plans
- possible issues in implementing marketing plans

4.1 The major components of marketing plans

An overview of marketing plans

A **marketing plan** is a document setting out the strategy a business will use to achieve its marketing objectives. The plan will include the following:
- Marketing targets that the firm is attempting to achieve.
- The elements of the marketing mix (place, price, promotion and product) to be used and how they will be coordinated.
- The timescale to which the plan relates (normally several years).
- The resources available to fund the marketing plan. This section will include a marketing budget (see below for more details on marketing budgets).

A marketing plan for a large organisation might bring together a number of separate marketing plans for individual goods and services.

Marketing budgets

A marketing budget is the amount of money that a business allocates for expenditure on marketing activities over a particular period of time. This money is likely to be used for a variety of activities, including advertising, sales promotions, public relations and market research.

The size of a firm's marketing budget is determined by a number of factors:
- **The financial position of the business.** If a business is recording rising profits, it is likely to be able to fund higher levels of expenditure on advertising and other marketing activities. However, it might be more sensible if a business spent more on marketing during less prosperous periods in order to increase sales and profits.
- **The actions of competitors.** If a business's rivals are increasing expenditure on marketing activities, it is likely that the firm in question will follow suit. For example, the marketing budgets of the businesses competing in the market for package holidays will rise together. Marketing, and especially advertising, is an important form of competition in many markets.
- **The business's marketing objectives.** If a firm has set objectives such as increasing market share or extending its product range, it is likely to spend heavily on marketing. Increasing market share might require substantial expenditure on advertising and sales promotions, while extending the product range may mean that the business has to invest in extensive market research.

Forecasting sales

Good forecasting is a key component of business success. Firms are likely to want to forecast data that relate to:

- sales of product(s)
- costs for the forthcoming accounting period
- cash flow
- key economic variables, such as inflation, unemployment, exchange rates and incomes

Time-series analysis involves forecasting future data from past figures. A firm is able to predict future sales by analysing its sales figures over previous years. This builds on work we did earlier on analysing trends using techniques such as extrapolation, moving averages and correlation (pages 30–32).

Analysis of a business's historic data can reveal patterns in those data. These patterns include the following:

- **Trends.** A trend is the underlying pattern of growth or decline in a series of data. Identifying a pattern in historic data will help the business to predict what will happen in the future. A trend can be identified by calculating and plotting the moving average using the technique explained on page 32. Establishing trends helps managers to forecast sales and to ensure they have sufficient resources available so that production can meet demand.
- **Seasonality.** This relates to shorter-term fluctuations arising from the time of year. Many businesses, pubs and wine merchants, for example, enjoy higher sales at Christmas. Travel agents expect peak sales in the spring and summer, and costs of vegetables for hotels and restaurants are lower in the summer.
- **Cycles.** These reflect periodic changes in patterns over a period of time. It is important for a firm to establish the reasons for these cycles. They may be related to fluctuations in the economy or successful (or unsuccessful) marketing activities. An example of the operation of cycles is in the building industry, which suffers severely from economic booms and recessions. In a recession, firms do not want new factories or offices, and fewer people purchase new homes.

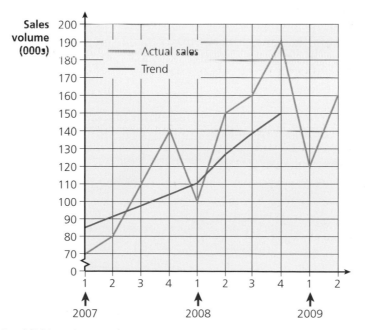

Figure 3.5 Establishing the trend

Why do firms forecast sales?

Businesses might choose to forecast sales for a variety of reasons:

- Sales forecasts form the basis of budgets for many businesses. From these figures, firms can plan production levels and draw up budgets that assist in the management of the enterprise. Sales forecasts also help businesses to predict the timing of income and expenditure, and to express this information in the form of cash-flow forecasts.
- Forecasts help firms to avoid overproduction and the possibility of selling off inventories (stock) at low (and perhaps unprofitable) prices. They also help to avoid unnecessary storage costs.
- Forecasting sales provides important information about changes in the market. If a competitor has introduced a product, or a new business has entered the market, a firm will benefit from an accurate assessment of the impact this change may have on its sales.

4.2 The major internal and external influences on marketing plans

There are a number of key influences on the marketing plan that a particular business may draw up:

- **The finance available to the business.** Initially this might appear to be an obvious influence on the marketing budget, but it can also influence the approach to sales forecasting (i.e. how extensive it is as well as the timescale and the specific marketing mix that is to be used). Access to more funds allows a business to set more expansive and challenging marketing objectives and to pursue them through extensive and expensive advertising campaigns and programmes of new product development.
- **Operational issues.** A business can only put in its marketing plan what it can actually deliver. Thus, the available operational resources will act as a constraint. For example, the productive capacity of the business may determine the number of markets in which the business can operate. Additionally, the cost at which the business can supply its products will be a key determinant of its pricing strategy and of the markets in which it thinks it can succeed. If it cannot compete on equal terms in, for example, the US market, its plan is likely to exclude this type of market development.
- **Competitors' actions.** It is common for businesses trading in markets that are dominated by a few large firms to consider the likely reactions of competitors as an integral part of planning. Businesses in such markets are said to be interdependent. In such circumstances, sales forecasts will be drawn up carefully and underpinned with assumptions about the likely responses of rivals. Similarly, the marketing budget will take into account the amount that competitors are expected to spend on marketing.

Examiner's tip

Don't forget that marketing plans are subject to influences from all the other functions within the business. A marketing plan should not include what the business cannot afford or what it cannot deliver because of human resource or operational problems.

4.3 Issues in implementing marketing plans

Marketing planning may be more important for a business that has recently started trading or for one considering a major change, such as entering a new market. A marketing plan may be more valuable for businesses whose markets are not volatile. This means that unexpected and significant changes will not ruin months of careful planning. Despite this, marketing plans do not always work as the planners had intended.

The benefits of marketing planning

Businesses can gain significant benefits from drawing up marketing plans:

● Plans help to give a sense of direction to all employees within the business.

● The business's managers can compare their achievement with the plan and take the necessary action if they are not on target.

● Planning is a worthwhile process in itself. It encourages managers to think ahead and to weigh up the options open to the firm as well as to consider threats and opportunities.

Potential problems in marketing planning

But plans have to be treated with caution too:

● Drawing up a marketing plan takes time and resources. In a rapidly changing marketplace, this might not be the optimal approach, as quick decisions (possibly based on hunches) might be required.

● Plans might encourage managers to be inflexible and not to respond to changes in the marketplace. Sometimes it might be more important to change the marketing targets than to achieve them.

CHAPTER 4 Operational strategies

Understanding operational objectives

What you need to know:
- the nature of operational objectives
- the internal and external influences on operational objectives

A business's operations function or department is responsible for the production of the good or service that the business supplies. This function was previously referred to as 'production'. This term is less used nowadays, as it tends to imply manufacturing rather than the broader remit of supplying goods and services.

1.1 The nature of operational objectives

Operational objectives are the targets pursued by the operations function or department of the business. The achievement of these goals should assist the business in attaining its corporate objectives. There are a number of operational objectives, the importance of which will vary according to the type of business, its products and the market in which it is trading.

Quality targets

A quality product is one that meets customers' needs fully. A firm that produces quality products is more likely to be considered a competitive business. A business may set itself a number of quality targets, such as:

- **A specific percentage of faulty products.** This type of target can be used in manufacturing and service contexts. For an insurance company it could relate to documentation with errors, while in a manufacturing context it could be goods that do not operate properly. A business may set a quality target of 1% faulty products, although it is not uncommon for businesses to set targets of zero defects.
- **The implementation of quality standards in a specific timescale.** Businesses may adopt quality standards, most notably ISO 9000. This is intended to assure customers that the business has appropriate procedures for ensuring the supply of quality products.

Cost and volume targets

- **Cost targets.** A business may set itself a **unit cost target**, aiming to produce its products at or below a stated average or unit cost. Meeting such a cost target allows the business more freedom in its pricing decisions and increases its competitiveness. This would be a particularly important operational target for budget airlines such as easyJet.
- **Volume targets.** These exist when a business plans to produce more than a certain amount of output. For example, a football club such as Tottenham Hotspur may aim for an average attendance in excess of 40,000 per match. This helps to increase market share and raise the profile of a business or brand, but it does not guarantee any profits because a low selling price may be necessary to achieve the target level of sales.

Innovation

Innovation is the creation of new ideas and the successful development of products from these ideas. It can also relate to new ways of making products. A business may set itself a target of being innovative and of bringing a certain number of new products

to the market each year. Innovation is more likely to be an operational target for businesses selling in fashion and technological markets.

Efficiency targets

An efficient business produces the maximum number of outputs (goods and services) with the minimum number of inputs (labour, capital, raw materials, fuel, time, etc.) Efficiency can take a number of forms:

- **Cost efficiency.** Firms pursuing this objective make products very cheaply, which may be highly attractive to certain groups of customers.
- **Resource efficiency.** Businesses may produce little waste as a consequence of the production process. This may involve recycling offcuts and any heat or water produced as a byproduct.
- **Time efficiency.** Japanese car manufacturers have a record of developing new products more quickly than many of their competitors. Bringing new advanced products to the market early allows them to gain **first mover advantage** and to benefit from a period of **premium pricing**. The Toyota Prius (a hybrid car) is a good example of the efficient management of time as it was the first hybrid car to be available.

Environmental targets

For many organisations, this type of operational target is assuming ever greater importance. For industries in the so-called 'polluting sector' (e.g. oil and chemical businesses), setting and meeting environmental targets is a vital aspect of the management of the business. Environmental targets can take a number of different forms, depending on the nature of the business:

- reducing or eliminating the use of non-sustainable resources
- reducing carbon emissions of the business's 'carbon footprint'
- cutting back on the amount of waste produced in the production process
- achieving targets for recycling — often expressed in terms of percentages

1.2 The internal and external influences on operational objectives

Internal influences

Internal influences on operational objectives may include:

- **The corporate objectives of the business.** The corporate and operations objectives of the business should be consistent and should not conflict. Thus, a business with a corporate objective of growth may seek to operate with cost targets as prime operational objectives to allow it to reduce prices in the expectation of increasing sales and market share. A business that wishes to develop a brand image of being environmentally friendly may have very different operational objectives.
- **The financial position of the business.** A business may not be able to afford to invest in machinery to meet self-imposed environmental targets if it has endured a poor trading period. Similarly, it may not be able to use recycled materials, which may be more expensive, in such circumstances.
- **The nature of the product.** For manufacturing firms, environmental issues and therefore targets may be given a higher priority. A business selling a luxury product is more likely to set targets in terms of quality, while time-based targets may be given prominence in the fashion industry.

External influences

External influences on operational objectives can take a number of forms:

- **The operations objectives of competitors.** It may be that consumers compare the products supplied by firms directly. For this reason, businesses may need to match the operational objectives of their rivals. It would be damaging for one of the UK's major oil companies to be seen to be more damaging to the environment than its competitors.
- **Legislation.** The UK government and the EU authorities have enacted laws that impact on the operational objectives that firms can set themselves. Most businesses supplying services are subject to safety laws designed to protect consumers. Thus, what can happen in the kitchen of a restaurant is governed by hygiene laws and this affects the production of food. In contrast, most businesses are subject to employment laws limiting the hours that they can require an employee to work each week. This has a considerable impact on the operations of all businesses.
- **Tastes and fashions.** A business may set itself time-based operational targets if it expects regular changes in the tastes and fashions of its customers. This enables it to meet their needs as soon as possible. In other industries, innovation may be important to meet the changing demands of the market.

2 Operational strategies: scale and resource mix

What you need to know:
- economies and diseconomies of scale
- capital and labour intensity

To operate efficiently it is necessary for a business to operate at the right scale – large enough to benefit from size, but not so large as to become unwieldy. Equally important is to use the right combination of resources of labour and capital. This topic considers these two issues.

2.1 Economies and diseconomies of scale

Economies of scale

As firms grow in size, they begin to benefit from **economies of scale**. This means that unit production costs fall and, up to a point, efficiency and profits improve. This offers businesses huge competitive advantages. Figure 4.1 illustrates this point.

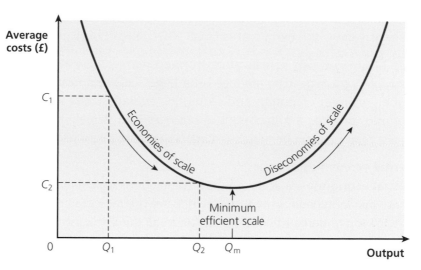

Figure 4.1 Economies and diseconomies of scale and minimum efficient scale

A firm that can only produce an output of $0Q_1$ will face a cost per unit of $0C_1$ and will have to set prices at this level (at least) or face a loss. A larger firm producing $0Q_2$ will be able to price around $0C_2$ and, depending on price elasticity of demand, may dominate the market.

If the firm's output exceeds the **minimum efficient scale** ($0Q_m$), it will face higher unit costs if it increases its scale of output. One reason why unit costs fall as output expands is that fixed costs are spread over more units of output.

Examiner's tip

When considering the benefits of economies of scale and lower unit costs, it is worth considering **price elasticity of demand**. Economies of scale allow businesses to reduce prices, and by incorporating price elasticity, a strong analytical line of argument may be constructed.

Economies of scale can be split into two types: internal and external.

Internal economies of scale

Internal economies of scale are those factors that reduce average costs in an individual firm as it increases the scale of its operations. Examples include the following:

- **Purchasing economies**, which exist when firms are able to buy components and materials more cheaply, taking advantage of bulk discounts. They may also employ trained buyers who can negotiate the best deals.
- **Production economies**, which arise from the use of mass production techniques to speed up production. Firms producing greater quantities can afford to buy large, specialised, technically advanced machinery to lower production costs.
- **Risk-bearing economies**, which mean that larger businesses can afford to take risks when launching new products and even sustain losses to a limited degree. Such businesses can also operate an R&D department.
- **Financial economies**, which mean that larger enterprises can borrow more easily and at more favourable rates of interest, as they have greater reserves. Financial specialists may also be able to advise them on how to reduce costs further.

- **Marketing economies**, which reduce unit costs because firms can afford to advertise extensively — the extra cost is small when spread over many units of output.

Some businesses can benefit more from economies of scale than others. Firms with heavy fixed costs need to produce on a large scale to spread these costs over a large number of units of output and to reduce average costs to a minimum. Similarly, economies of scale are important to businesses in fiercely price-competitive markets. This is a major reason behind the mergers that have taken place between supermarkets.

External economies of scale

External economies of scale are the advantages of scale that benefit the whole industry and not just individual firms. So, if an industry is concentrated in one geographical area, the following benefits might be available to all the firms involved:
- a network of suitable and established suppliers
- a pool of skilled labour
- training courses arranged at local colleges
- a suitable infrastructure — roads, rail links, etc.

Diseconomies of scale

Large firms can suffer from **diseconomies of scale**. Once they are past their minimum efficient scale, the cost per unit of production begins to increase. This may be due to:
- **Over-use of existing machinery.** This increases maintenance costs and causes breakdowns.
- **Communication problems.** As the business grows, people may not know whom to report to. Managers may begin to rely on sending memos rather than speaking to people directly.
- **Marketing problems.** Managers may not concentrate on the right products.

The fact that large businesses are not necessarily more profitable than small or medium-sized businesses is evidence that diseconomies of scale do operate in the real world. The optimum size of a business may also change over time as the market, personnel and technology change.

Examiner's tip

It is often argued that economies of scale are technical in origin, while diseconomies arise from problems with people (e.g. communications). There is potential for a powerful line of analysis in this distinction.

2.2 Capital and labour intensity

Capital-intensive production occurs when the production of the good or service relies more heavily on capital (e.g. equipment and machinery) than on other factors of production. **Labour-intensive production** relies more heavily on the use of labour.

Choosing the resource mix

Deciding on the right mix of labour and capital can be a tricky decision and depends on a number of factors:
- **The size of the business.** It may be that a larger firm is able to justify using (and can afford to use) types of technology in its production that a smaller business would not

employ. Thus, large-scale car manufacturers such as Nissan operate production lines that rely heavily on computer-controlled robots. On the other hand, Lotus, the sports car manufacturer, relies much more on skilled labour as a key component of its production process.

- **The type of product.** If a business produces large quantities of standard products, it may be feasible to use a greater proportion of capital in the production process. This would not be a sensible choice for a business that produces more individual products made to the order of specific customers. Some service industries, such as health and education, rely heavily on labour because only limited suitable technology is available.
- **The finance available to the business.** Adopting capital-intensive production systems can be an expensive option. Not only does the business have to invest in the capital equipment, but it may also face substantial expenditure in training its employees to use the equipment efficiently. A further cost may be incurred if it has to make some employees redundant (as they are to be replaced by capital equipment) and has to pay compensation.

Advantages and disadvantages

Both capital- and labour-intensive systems of production have advantages and disadvantages.

Labour-intensive production can lead to substantial costs in terms of recruitment, selection and training. This can become a large burden if the business suffers from a high rate of labour turnover. It is also possible that labour disputes will lead to a serious disruption in production. On the plus side, labour-intensive production may allow the business to claim a unique selling point ('hand-made' products) and to be more flexible in meeting the precise needs of customers.

Capital-intensive production may help businesses to reduce their unit costs and to produce standard goods that meet agreed specifications, including quality targets. Capital-intensive businesses may be more flexible in terms of quantity of output, as the machinery can be operated for longer or shorter periods as desired. However, machinery can be expensive and there is a danger that the technology either is unreliable or becomes obsolescent more quickly than expected.

3 *Operational strategies: innovation*

What you need to know:
- the meanings of innovation and research and development
- the purpose, costs, benefits and risk of innovation

3.1 Innovation and research and development

Innovation is the creation of new ideas and the successful development of products from these ideas. Innovation can also relate to new ways of making products. **Research and development** (R&D) is scientific investigation leading to new ideas for products and the development of those ideas into products. Innovation tends to have a slightly broader meaning, in that it includes the creation of a commercially successful product.

Innovation is vital in industries such as pharmaceuticals, which spend enormous sums of money on developing new products. The same is true of any technologically based industry, including computer hardware and software as well as the growing biotechnology industries.

3.2 The purpose, costs, benefits and risk of innovation

The purpose of innovation

Innovation takes place before a product is launched, that is, before the commencement of the product life cycle. This may result in the business facing difficulties with its cash flow. However, a successful business may be able to subsidise new products from more established ones (cash cows).

When a product enters the growth and maturity stages of the life cycle, however, it might be appropriate to invest in innovation for the next generation of products. This may need to occur even earlier if the new products are likely to take time to develop. In the case of some pharmaceutical products, it can take up to 20 years to turn an idea into a commercial product.

The purpose of innovation is to give a business a competitive edge. Bringing successful new products onto the market before those of rivals allows a company to develop its reputation and to charge premium prices, thereby boosting profits. Apple is a prime example of a successful innovative company.

Benefits of innovation

The benefits of innovation include:
- Businesses can gain a significant competitive advantage by being the first to bring a new product onto the market. Sony achieved high sales and profits when it introduced the first personal stereo. A high-technology product with no direct rivals allows firms to charge high prices (price skimming). This had a positive impact on the company's profits.
- Businesses can gain a reputation for producing high-quality and sophisticated products. This image can boost sales of other, related products.
- Patents can be used to protect business ideas for up to 20 years, allowing inventors to generate substantial earnings from their research and innovation. Many companies (e.g. Guinness) allow other businesses to produce their products in other parts of the world under licence.

Disadvantages of innovation

Innovation also has the following costs:
- Research can be very expensive and only large firms can afford to engage in it. Pharmaceutical firms spend many millions of pounds developing new products and only a tiny proportion of their ideas result in successful products.
- The timescale can be lengthy, meaning that investors have to wait a long time for a return on their money. This may not be viable unless the business has other profitable products on the market at the same time.
- Other companies may adopt 'me too' products that are similar (but not too similar) to a product resulting from expensive research. These 'me too' products will enjoy some of the sales associated with the original product. Friends Reunited is a successful website, but a number of rivals soon appeared.
- To succeed in highly competitive markets, firms must continuously innovate and sell new products. It is not enough to have a single successful product, since at some point sales will decline as newer, more advanced products enter the market.

Innovation and risk

There are two main reasons why a strategy of innovation can be risky:

- **The innovative product may fail.** About one in a hundred ideas developed in the pharmaceutical industry actually makes it onto the market. This means that firms spend enormous sums of money on projects that do not generate any returns. If the proportion of unsuccessful products increases, the business may experience financial problems.

- **Other firms may copy the idea.** We saw above how rivals copy innovative products. This can be a major problem for a business that has incurred all the research and development costs without getting the benefits of selling large numbers of premium-priced products. However, businesses can protect their ideas by using the forms of protection provided by the law.

Businesses can protect their ideas in a number of ways:

- **Patents** provide protection for products and processes for up to 20 years. A new processor for computers might have a patent on it.

- **Copyrights** provide protection for the creators and owners of literary, dramatic musical and artistic works. They can last for up to 70 years after the death of the author and are granted automatically. They apply to books, music and cartoons.

- **Trademarks** grant legal ownership of recognisable signs and symbols for an indefinite period. Firms such as Adidas use trademarks to protect their symbols, and Perrier prevents rivals copying the shape and colour of the bottles in which it sells mineral water. The 1994 Trade Marks Act brought UK legislation in this area into line with the EU.

4   Operational strategies: location

What you need to know:

- methods of making location decisions
- the benefits of optimal location
- issues in multi-site and international location decisions

4.1 Methods of making location decisions

Location decisions are becoming critical as more and more businesses sell their products in global markets. Taking location decisions is likely to require the application of important quantitative techniques:

- **Investment appraisal techniques.** Payback, average rate of return and discounted cash-flow techniques may assist managers in making objective choices between two or more locations. The site that offers the speediest return on the initial investment, or the greatest return over, say, a 10-year period, may be thought the most appealing.

- **Break-even analysis.** Another method of comparison may be to choose the site that requires the lowest level of output and sales to break even.

The factors influencing location

Although quantitative techniques may play an important part in the decision, ultimately the judgement is likely to be based on a mixture of qualitative and quantitative factors. This is not uncommon in business.

- **Power and raw materials.** Primary industry, such as mining and other extractive industries, has to be located near to raw materials. Deposits of raw materials, such as coal, iron ore and oil, determine the location of these industries. Such 'traditional' factors are of limited importance in modern location decisions. Gas and electricity are available in almost all parts of the UK, and modern transport systems now carry goods cheaply and efficiently throughout the country.

- **Markets.** The location of many firms is determined by their need to be close to their markets. According to Weber's Law, businesses which produce goods that are more bulky than the raw materials used to make them are likely to locate close to their markets. The components and materials used to brew beer, for example, are far less bulky than the final product because of the water that is added during the brewing process. Suppliers of components and intermediate goods may set up close to their major customers.

- **Suitably skilled labour.** Firms relocating may take most of their existing staff with them. This helps to reduce disruption and the expense of recruiting new staff. There are shortages of particular skills among the labour force in certain areas of the UK, while some regions have labour forces that possess certain skills. For example, a firm considering food processing might find Norfolk attractive because a suitably trained labour force already exists there. Where an industry is already concentrated in a particular region, advantages are often available, such as research facilities in nearby universities and established suppliers of components. We encountered such **external economies of scale** earlier.

- **Infrastructure.** Transport and communication links are important to many businesses; hence many firms locate near to motorways.

- **Government influence.** The government offers considerable assistance to firms locating in specific areas of the UK. Regional Selective Assistance (RSA) is paid in instalments to firms that create employment in designated areas. They can claim for expenditure on land, buildings, plant and machinery. Local authority assistance might include grants, loans or guarantees for borrowing. Local authorities may also invest directly in the business. The Single Regeneration Budget, financed by the European Union, provides support for economic development and to promote competitiveness in depressed areas. In recent years, proposals have had to demonstrate that they are environmentally friendly. Finally, Enterprise Areas, announced in the Budget of 2002, are small, deprived, inner-city areas into which the government is hoping to attract businesses by reducing bureaucracy and offering financial incentives, such as supporting private investment with government cash.

In addition there are two other major EU sources of funds are available:

- The **European Regional Development Fund** aims to reduce regional differences in prosperity and assist disadvantaged regions, particularly run-down areas facing industrial decline as well as impoverished rural areas.

- The **European Social Fund** aims to improve employment opportunities in the EU by providing financial support towards the running costs for vocational training schemes, guidance and counselling projects as well as general job creation measures.

4.2 The benefits of an optimal location

Most businesses seek to minimise costs when taking location decisions. To do otherwise would mean that competitiveness would be reduced and profits diminished. Increasingly, location decisions also have an international dimension as companies seek to trade throughout world markets. An optimal location can reduce unit costs in a number of ways:

- **By offering lower labour costs.** This can be particularly important for businesses where labour costs represent a high proportion of total costs.
- **By reducing administrative costs.** There may be fewer laws in some countries with which a business has to comply. This can streamline the production process and reduce costs.
- **By avoiding tariffs (taxes on imports).** Many Asian manufacturers locate in the UK to avoid having to pay tariffs when exporting their products to the EU.

However, optimal locations can offer businesses other benefits too:

- **Access to the latest research facilities.** Some high-technology businesses opt to locate on university research parks. This gives them the benefit of easy access to the university's research facilities.
- **High-calibre staff.** An optimal location may enable a business to attract high-quality staff with the right skills. It is not just a question of cost for businesses that require large numbers of highly trained employees.
- **A prestigious address.** For some businesses (fashion houses, merchant banks and some retailers) an address in an expensive part of London or other major city might be a vital element in marketing the business.

4.3 Issues in multi-site and international location decisions

Throughout the developed world, the size of firms is growing, principally through mergers. This means that an increasing number of firms have locations in more than one country. Businesses that operate (as opposed to just selling) in more than one country are known as **multinationals**.

Multi-site location

It is not unusual for large businesses to operate on more than one site. This can be within a single country or in many countries. We consider the issues involved in operating as a multinational in more detail below. Many well-known UK businesses (e.g. Waitrose, Barclays Bank) operate many branches. Other businesses (e.g. Norwich Union, now part of the larger Aviva group) operate on a smaller number of larger sites.

Multi-site location creates a number of advantages and disadvantages. The major advantages are set out below.

- A multi-site location permits a business to be closer to its markets and to monitor market trends better. Thus, fashion clothing stores that operate throughout the UK can research local markets on an ongoing basis.
- Multi-site location can give a business a prestigious address as well as the benefits of cheaper sites elsewhere.
- Some large businesses are in effect several smaller businesses operating as a conglomerate. Having a number of locations allows each element of the business to be in its optimal location.

- Multi-site location encourages a greater degree of delegation and empowerment, which can enhance motivation and employee performance.
- It can allow the firm to operate on a large scale without all the potential problems of diseconomies of scale.

These advantages are balanced to a greater or lesser extent by the disadvantages:

- Communication is more problematic, as employees may be unable to meet face to face.
- The business may incur greater operating costs if materials need to be transported between the various sitcs.
- It may be necessary to relocate employees from one site to another, which could meet with resistance from those who are settled with family ties in a particular location.
- With multi-site location the business may be unable to take full advantage of economies of scale. There may, for example, be some duplication of administrative functions, leading to higher costs of production.

International location

International location operates on exactly the same principles as domestic location theory. Multinationals seek the lowest-cost location to maximise profits. Governments often offer incentives, such as grants and benefits, to multinationals for locating in their countries. The UK spends considerable sums of money to attract inward investment into the country.

Multinationals seek the following when taking location decisions:

- effective communications systems and transport networks
- trained and productive labour, available at relatively low rates of pay
- low rates of taxation levied on business profits
- local and national government grants to support the heavy investment necessary
- support services (e.g. components, research facilities) readily available

In addition, they consider a number of other factors:

- **Political stability.** A firm does not want to risk any disruption of its activities.
- **The need to avoid adverse exchange rate fluctuations.** This might be an argument for locating in countries using the euro. Some Asian car manufacturers have suggested that they might move from the UK to continental European countries, using the euro to remove the risk of adverse exchange rate fluctuations.
- **The need to avoid tariffs or other trade barriers.** One of the attractions for foreign businesses of locating in the UK is that they are able to trade within the EU's common external tariff.

Location is particularly important to some businesses in maintaining their competitiveness, especially if they employ large numbers of relatively unskilled workers. In recent years, famous UK manufacturers Dyson (vacuum cleaners) and Hornby (toys) have moved overseas to benefit from lower wage costs. Without these moves, they argued, they would have been unable to compete in terms of price with foreign businesses.

5 Operational strategies: lean production

What you need to know:
- how businesses manage time effectively
- the value of critical path analysis
- the other elements of lean production

The concept of **lean production** is increasingly used to describe the organisational goals of manufacturing industry. Sometimes called the 'Japanese approach', lean production describes a range of measures designed to use fewer inputs and resources. The measures include:
- cell production
- just-in-time production
- kaizen or continuous improvement
- benchmarking against market leaders
- time-based management and simultaneous engineering

5.1 How businesses manage time effectively

Time-based management

Time-based management seeks to shorten all aspects of production to reduce costs and make it easier to meet the needs of consumers. This type of management requires:
- flexible machinery that can be switched easily and quickly to new models and products
- multiskilled employees who can turn their hands to a variety of tasks, reducing delays and production costs
- heavy expenditure on training to ensure employees have sufficient and up-to-date skills

Lean producers are characterised by short product development times. Japanese car producers typically take 48 months from the first idea for a new vehicle to it becoming available to customers. In comparison, UK car manufacturers take 59 months.

Having short product development times offers a number of benefits:
- It may prove less costly, as less time and resources are devoted to research and development.
- A firm that is first to launch a product onto the market can charge a higher price (price skimming) and enjoy higher profits. This is particularly useful if demand is price inelastic.
- The position of market leader in this respect can motivate the workforce, so improving performance and profits.

Simultaneous engineering

Simultaneous engineering manages the development of new products in the shortest possible time. Some aspects of product development can be carried out at the same time, allowing products onto the market faster, cutting costs and generating revenue earlier than would otherwise have been the case.

Time is an important competitive weapon in industries where products are relatively undifferentiated and the same or similar technology is available to most businesses. Thus, manufacturers of vacuum cleaners strive to be the first to introduce new technology, so they can enjoy a brief period of superiority and premium pricing.

Critical path analysis

Critical path analysis (CPA) is a method of calculating and illustrating how complex projects can be completed as quickly as possible. CPA shows:

- the sequence in which the activities must be undertaken
- the length of time taken by each activity
- the earliest time at which each activity can commence
- the latest times at which each activity must be completed to avoid delaying later stages

It offers substantial benefits to businesses in planning the most efficient use of their resources. This can help to minimise costs and enhance competitiveness.

A CPA network consists of two elements, shown in Figure 4.2:

- **Activities.** These, shown by arrows, are the part of a project requiring time and probably the firm's resources. The arrows (running from left to right) show the sequence of the activities. They are frequently given letters to denote the order. The duration of each activity is written below the arrow. Some (but not all) activities cannot be started until others are concluded.
- **Nodes.** These are the start or finish of an activity and are represented by circles. Each node is numbered (in the left-hand segment) and also states the 'earliest start time' (EST) and 'latest finish time' (LFT).

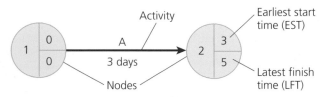

Figure 4.2 Activities and nodes in critical path analysis

An example of critical path analysis

A company is planning to increase capacity by extending its factory. The expansion is expected to cause disruption and the management team is keen to complete it as quickly as possible. The building firm has listed the major activities it will carry out as well as the expected duration of each.

Activity	Expected duration (weeks)
A Design the factory extension	6
B Obtain planning permission	4
C Dig and lay foundations	3
D Order construction materials	2
E Construct walls and roof	12
F Design interior	2
G Install production equipment	6
H Train staff in new techniques	16

The building firm has also provided the following information:

- Activity A is the start of the project.
- B starts when A is complete.

- C, D and F follow B.
- E follows C and D.
- H follows B.
- G follows F.

The network for the factory extension is shown in Figure 4.3.

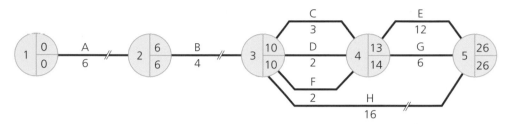

Figure 4.3 The network for the factory extension

The **critical path** shows the sequence of activities that must be completed on time if the whole project is not to be delayed. It is indicated by two small dashes across the relevant activities. In Figure 4.3 the critical path is A-B-H.

Earliest start times and latest finish times

The network in Figure 4.3 shows the earliest start times (ESTs) and latest finish times (LFTs) in the nodes.

- **Earliest start time.** The EST shows the earliest time at which a particular activity can be commenced. ESTs are calculated by working from left to right and adding the times taken to complete the previous activity. If there is more than a single activity, the activity with the longest duration is included in the calculation. The EST is recorded in the top of the two quadrants in the right-hand half of the node. The EST at node 4 is 13 days. This is because although activities D and F are complete after 12 days, activity E cannot commence until both C and D are complete. C is not complete until the end of day 13. The EST on the final node shows the earliest date at which the whole project can be concluded.
- **The latest finishing time.** The LFT records the time by which an activity must be completed if the entire project is not to be delayed. LFTs are calculated from right to left. From each LFT the activity with the longest duration is deducted. The LFT at node 3 is 10 days — the 26 days from node 5 less the 16 days of activity H. Calculating LFTs helps to highlight those activities in which there is some slack time or float.

The critical path

Those nodes in which EST = LFT (i.e. there is no float time) denote the critical path. The critical path:

- comprises those activities that take longest to complete
- allows managers to focus on those activities that must not be delayed for fear of delaying the entire project
- helps managers identify where additional resources might be needed to avoid any possibility of overrunning on projects

Float time

Float time is spare time that exists within a project. Thus, if an activity that takes 5 days has an allowance of 7 days in a network, 2 days of float time exist. In Figure 4.3, if activity E were delayed by 1 day, there would be no impact upon the entire project.

There are two types of float:

- **Total float.** Total float is the reserve time available for an activity. This can be used without delaying the entire project. Subtracting the duration of an activity from the LFT and then subtracting the EST gives the total float. The formula to calculate total float is:

  total float = LFT (current activity) – duration – EST (current activity)

- **Free float.** This is the amount of time by which an individual activity can be delayed without affecting any following activity. The formula is:

  free float = EST (following activity) – duration – EST (current activity)

Examiner's tip

In the examination you will not be expected to draw a critical path network from scratch. However, you may have to amend one or to add in LFTs and ESTs. You should therefore ensure that you understand the way in which the networks operate.

5.2 The value of critical path analysis

The value of critical path analysis in any situation depends on the extent to which the advantages outweigh the disadvantages, if they do. The assessment of value needs to be carried out on a case-by-case basis.

Advantages

- CPA encourages managers to undertake detailed planning, which helps to reduce the risk of delays and other problems.
- The resources needed for each activity can be made available at the appropriate time, reducing costs as well as improving the business's cash-flow position.
- Time can be saved by operating certain activities simultaneously. This can be vital in industries where time is an important competitive weapon.
- If delays and problems do occur, the network will assist in working out a solution.

Disadvantages

- Complex activities may be impossible to represent on a network.
- The project still requires management even after the initial network is drawn, as external factors may change.
- Much depends upon how accurately the durations of activities are estimated. These can be difficult to forecast and, if they are wrong, the whole process may be of little value.
- This third weakness led the US government, when developing the Polaris missile in the 1960s, to develop a system of estimating durations based on probabilities. This technique became known as 'programme evaluation and review technique' (PERT).

5.3 The other elements of lean production

We saw earlier that the term 'lean production' encompasses a range of techniques that a business may adopt. We consider some of these below.

Cell production

Cell production divides the activities on the production line into a series of independent units. Each of these units, known as **cells**, is self-contained. The idea, which originated in the Soviet Union, is intended to improve quality and motivation. Each cell should have a team leader supported by a number of multiskilled staff.

Quality is likely to be improved because later cells can become the customers of earlier cells and will reject any substandard items. This imposes a regular and rigorous check on quality and reduces the chance of customers receiving poor-quality products.

Motivation can also be enhanced because employees are given the authority to check their own work to ensure quality. In addition, working in a cell means that employees are involved in producing a complete product (even if it is only a component). Seeing an outcome of their efforts can stimulate workers to improve their performance.

Cell production usually operates alongside the just-in-time approach to production.

Just-in-time manufacturing

Just-in-time (JIT) manufacturing is a Japanese management philosophy that involves having the right items of the right quality in the right place at the right time. JIT is a central component of lean production.

The initial ideas originated in Japanese shipyards in an attempt to reduce the huge sums of money tied up in raw materials. JIT was developed and perfected in the Toyota factories by Taiichi Ohno as a means of meeting consumer demands with minimal costs and delays. Taiichi Ohno is often called the 'father' of JIT.

In the 1960s, Toyota worked hard on developing a whole range of new approaches to manufacturing. The oil crisis of the early 1970s accelerated this process and other Japanese manufacturers copied Toyota. In Japan, work takes precedence over leisure — it is common for people to work 14-hour days. This cultural feature not only encouraged the development of JIT, but also helped to ensure its subsequent success.

Just-in-time manufacturing is not one technique or even a set of techniques, but an overall philosophy embracing both old and new techniques. The philosophy is based on eliminating waste. Waste means anything other than the minimum level of equipment, materials, parts, space and workers' time. Thus JIT means using the minimum amount of resources to satisfy customer demand.

To comprehend JIT fully, it is important to distinguish between value added and non-value added activities in the business:

- **Value added activities** are those that convert the raw materials and components as part of the manufacturing process. These activities occur on the production line.
- **Non-value added activities** are those where the raw materials, components or finished products are not being worked on. Examples are storage and repairing faulty products.

Japanese firms employing JIT focus on reducing the time spent on non-value added activities, thus eliminating waste. Traditional UK management has concentrated on making value added activities more productive through methods such as work-study. In a typical UK factory, a product spends 95% of its time in non-value added activities. At these times, the product earns nothing yet still incurs costs.

It is usual to measure the level of waste in an organisation by measuring inventory levels. High inventory levels tend to hide quality problems, scrap, machine down-times and late deliveries. JIT is designed to highlight such issues.

The key characteristics of JIT are set out below.

- It is based on demand-pull production — demand signals when a product should be manufactured. Use of demand-pull enables a firm to produce only what is required in the appropriate quantity and at the correct time.
- Suppliers of components and other materials must be very responsive to orders from the manufacturer.
- It allows a reduction in raw materials, work-in-progress and finished goods inventories. This frees up a greater amount of space in factories.
- The layout of the factory is arranged for maximum worker flexibility, encouraging the use of multiskilled employees.
- It requires high levels of training to give workers the skills necessary to carry out a number of tasks.
- Employees engage in self-inspection to ensure that their products are of high quality and that value has been added.
- Continuous improvement is an integral part of JIT.

Kaizen

Kaizen means 'continuous improvement' and is an important element of lean production. It entails continual but small advances in production techniques, each improving productivity a little. The cumulative effect of these small improvements is shown in Figure 4.4.

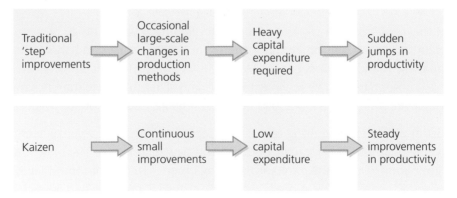

Figure 4.4 The contrast between continuous improvements under lean production and traditional 'step' improvements in productivity

The key features of kaizen are as follows:

- Kaizen groups meet regularly to discuss problems and to propose new ideas to improve productivity.
- The improvements proposed under the kaizen system cost relatively little but can have a substantial impact on costs of production.
- Mass production has traditionally relied on larger investments to improve technology. This involves great expense, partly in paying for redundancies, and large-scale changes take time to become effective. Lean production invites shop-floor ideas to produce regular and small-scale improvements in productivity, which are less likely to create job losses and damage morale.

The implementation of a policy of kaizen has considerable implications for a business's workforce:

- All employees should be continually seeking ways to improve their performance. This may involve new approaches and techniques, which could be relatively minor. Since employees are 'experts' at their jobs, they are best suited to generating effective ideas.
- Team working is an integral element of continuous improvement. Teams can be the basis of kaizen groups designed to provide ideas and solve problems.
- Empowerment gives employees control over their working lives. Empowered employees will feel confident in proposing ideas and have the authority to implement their decisions.
- Training is an important component of kaizen. Employees need new skills if they are to fulfil a number of roles within the team. Training will also assist teams in planning their work and implementing their decisions with minimal disruption of production.
- Senior management in a business employing kaizen must ensure that the culture of the organisation is conducive to empowered teams planning their work and taking decisions to improve productivity. All managers must subscribe to the company's philosophy.

Inevitably, kaizen has some potential shortcomings:

- Traditional managers may resist its implementation, as it reduces their power and control in the organisation.
- Some people argue that the impact of kaizen diminishes over time. This is partly because the more obvious ideas and improvements are implemented early on and partly because employee enthusiasm dwindles over time.
- Industries that experience regular changes in consumer tastes and fashions may not be so well suited to kaizen. The fashion industry, for example, requires major rethinks on a regular basis to maintain consumer interest.

1 Understanding human resource objectives and strategies

What you need to know:
- the nature of human resource (HR) objectives
- the internal and external influences on HR objectives
- the major HR strategies

A business's human resource function or department is responsible for the use of labour within the organisation. This is a wide-ranging function involving activities from recruitment to setting HR objectives and HR strategies.

1.1 The nature of HR objectives

Human resource objectives are the targets pursued by the HR function or department of the business. The achievement of these goals should assist the business is attaining its corporate objectives. There are a number of HR objectives, the importance of which will vary according to the type of business, its products and the market in which it is trading.

Matching the workforce to the needs of the business
It is normal for the labour needs of a business to change over time. A business might grow, move overseas, replace employees with technology or take a decision to produce new products. Each of these actions means that the business will require a different workforce. This might require the HR department to recruit new employees, make employees redundant and redeploy employees to a new location, or to train employees to provide the necessary skills.

Meeting this objective allows the firm to be as competitive as possible because its workforce is the right size and has the required skills. Fulfilling this objective requires ongoing action on the part of the HR function.

Making full use of the workforce's potential
A workforce's potential exists in a number of forms:
- **Skills.** It is possible that employees have some skills which they do not use as part of their working lives. For example, a manager might be fluent in a second language. Businesses can use skills audits to identify such skills and then make use of them as and when appropriate.
- **Underutilised employees.** Some employees may find that their jobs are not really challenging. They may not stretch them or utilise their talents to their full extent. On the other hand, some employees may not have sufficient work to occupy them fully. Identifying and responding effectively to such circumstances will improve the performance of the workforce.
- **Overworked or stressed employees.** The opposite circumstance can occur, especially if a business is seeking to reduce its operating costs. This can result in employees having excessive workloads or being asked to take positions in the organisation for which they are not properly trained or qualified.

Maintaining good employer–employee relations

Maintaining good relations with employees is an important HR objective for most businesses. Good employer–employee relations offer businesses a range of benefits:

- It makes costly strikes and other labour disputes less likely.
- Research has shown that businesses with good industrial relations attract higher-calibre and better-qualified applicants for positions.
- Good employer–employee relations assist a business in maintaining a positive corporate image, which may have a positive effect on sales.
- In such circumstances, employer–employee communications may be effective in helping to resolve problems and encouraging suggestions for improving production.

1.2 The internal and external influences on HR objectives

Internal influences on HR objectives

There are a number of internal factors which may influence a business's decision on which HR objectives to pursue. They include:

- **Corporate objectives.** As with all functional objectives, those set by the HR department must assist the organisation in achieving its overall objectives. If the business has a corporate objective of maximising long-term profits, the HR function might set itself objectives concerned with reducing labour costs or making the most effective use of the workforce.
- **The attitudes and beliefs of the senior managers.** The senior managers of a business can have an important influence on HR objectives. If they consider the workforce to be a valuable asset, they may want a long-term relationship with employees and may set objectives such as developing the skills of the workforce to their fullest extent. Alternatively, they may see employees as an expendable asset to be hired when necessary and paid the minimum rate possible.
- **The type of product.** If the product requires the commitment of a highly skilled labour force (as in the case of healthcare), objectives such as making the full use of the workforce's potential may be most important. However, for businesses selling products that are mainly produced by machinery and require little in the way of skilled labour, minimising labour costs may be a key HR objective.

External influences on HR objectives

External factors will have a significant impact on the HR objectives that are set by businesses.

- **Price elasticity of demand for the product.** When demand for a product is strongly price elastic (i.e. demand is very sensitive to price changes), it is more likely that a business will opt for HR objectives that allow it to reduce labour costs. This can be seen in the case of budget airlines.
- **Corporate image.** Most businesses will set HR objectives that include maintaining good relations with employees. To become embroiled in an industrial dispute can be damaging to the image of a business and may lead to a loss in sales.
- **Employment legislation.** The UK government and EU authorities have passed a series of laws designed to protect labour in the workplace. The existence of such laws may encourage businesses to set HR objectives to develop the potential of their workforce, as the law may make it difficult and/or expensive to hire and fire employees at will.

1.3 The major HR strategies

Since the 1970s, many firms have abandoned **personnel management** in favour of **human resource management** (HRM). Personnel management encompassed tasks such as recruitment and selection, training, discipline, pay and employee records. This approach viewed each of these tasks as discrete functions and personnel management was not considered to be a strategic function. It was not uncommon for personnel management to be overseen by a middle manager.

The adoption of HRM has elevated the status of people who manage people and has encouraged the devising and adoption of HR strategies to be implemented across the organisation.

Making the most effective use of the workforce has become a strategic function, headed by a senior manager or a director. It also integrates all elements of managing people to ensure that the approach is coordinated.

Businesses have adopted HRM for a number of reasons:
- In the Western economies, most firms supply services. In service industries, the quality of employees is an important competitive weapon. Making the most effective use of the workforce can assist in boosting profits and achieving other corporate objectives.
- Companies using HRM have appeared to manage their workforces more effectively and have become more competitive as a consequence. Other businesses have therefore imitated this approach.
- The process of reducing the number of layers of hierarchy in the organisation and the delegation of authority have meant that managers further down the organisational hierarchy have taken more decisions in relation to employees. The philosophy of HRM fits in with this approach.

Not all businesses take the same view of HR strategies. Two broad approaches have emerged (see Table 6.1).
- **'Hard' HR approach.** The 'hard' approach to HR strategies views employees as a resource to be used as efficiently as possible; in this way they are no different from vehicles or production machinery. Employees are hired as cheaply as possible, managed closely and made redundant when no longer required.
- **'Soft' HR approach**. The 'soft' approach is based on the belief that employees are perhaps the most valuable asset a business possesses. Thus, it is in the business's interest to maximise their value to the organisation. Employees are valued and developed over time and help to make a business competitive in the marketplace.

2 *Developing and implementing workforce plans*

What you need to know:
- the components of workforce plans
- the internal and external influences on workforce plans
- issues in workforce planning
- the value of workforce planning

	'Hard' HR approach	**'Soft' HR approach**
Philosophy	Employees are no different from any other resource used by the business.	Employees are the most valuable resource available to the business and a vital competitive weapon.
Timescale	HRM operates in the short term only: employees are hired and fired as necessary.	Employees are developed over a long period of time to help the firm fulfil its corporate objectives.
Key features	• Pay is kept to a minimum. • Little or no empowerment. • Communication is mainly downwards. • Leaders have a Theory X view of employees. • Emphasis is on the short term in recruiting and training employees.	• Employees are empowered and encouraged to take decisions. • Leaders have a Theory Y view of workforce • Employees are encouraged to extend and update skills. • Employees are consulted regularly by managers. • A long-term relationship is developed with employees through use of internal recruitment and ongoing training programmes.
Associated leadership style	This approach is more likely to be adopted by leaders using an autocratic style of leadership.	This approach is more likely to be adopted by leaders using a democratic style of leadership.
Motivational techniques used	Principally financial techniques with minimal use of techniques such as delegation.	Techniques intended to give employees more control over their working lives, e.g. delegation and empowered teams.

Table 5.1 'Hard' and 'soft' HR strategies

2.1 The components of workforce plans

Planning the most effective use of human resources is an important element in meeting corporate objectives. Businesses have to decide on the amount and type of labour that they will require, given their objectives and the anticipated level of sales.

Those responsible for HR draw up a **workforce plan** to detail the number and type of workers the business needs to recruit as well as any necessary redeployments, redundancies and retraining. The plan also specifies how the business will implement its workforce plan. An important element of this is a **skills audit** to identify the abilities and qualities of the existing workforce, highlighting skills and talents within the workforce of which managers were unaware.

Businesses require specific information for their development of workforce plans (see Figure 5.1 overleaf).

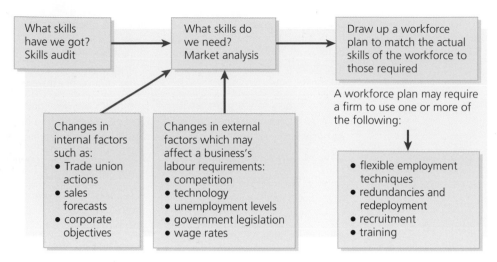

Figure 5.1 *Workforce planning*

A business's workforce plan will contain the following information:

- Information on the business's current workforce: size, skills, locations, age profile, etc.
- An analysis of likely changes in the demand for the business's products and hence in the business's need for labour in the forthcoming period.
- An analysis of the likely factors affecting the supply of labour: forecast rates of labour turnover for the business and factors affecting the local labour markets.
- Recommendations as to the actions the firm needs to take to acquire and retain the desired workforce. These might include recruitment, training, redeployment and redundancy.

A workforce plan will allow the company to use its human resources effectively and at minimum cost in pursuit of its corporate objectives.

2.2 The internal and external influences on workforce plans

There are a wide range of external and internal influences on workforce plans:

- **Sales forecasts.** Estimating sales for the next year or two can be a prime influence on workforce plans. This helps the business to identify the quantity and type of labour the firm will require to meet the expected demand for its products.
- **Demographic trends.** The business also needs information on potential entrants to the labour force, which depends on demographic factors such as migration and birth rates.
- **Wage rates.** If wages are expected to rise, businesses may reduce their demand for labour and seek to make greater use of technology.
- **Technological developments.** Changes in technology will have an impact on planning the workforce, as they may reduce the need for unskilled or even skilled employees, while creating employment for those with technical skills.
- **Changes in legislation.** Employment laws can limit the number of hours employees may work each week or require businesses to offer employees benefits such as paternity leave. Such changes may mean that a business requires greater amounts of labour or may persuade it to replace labour with capital equipment.

2.3 Issues in workforce planning

Workforce planning does not take place in a vacuum. HR managers have to take a number of factors into account when drawing up workforce plans:

- **Employer–employee relations.** The business should not take decisions about the workforce without consulting the workforce. Indeed, EU legislation makes this a legal requirement for larger businesses. Reducing the size of the workforce through a programme of redundancy, if lower sales are forecast, might not reduce the organisation's costs. Such a strategy may result in an industrial dispute, leading to lost sales and the alienation of customers. This might not be in the long-term interest of the business.
- **Changes in technology.** New technology offers businesses different ways to meet the needs of their customers. For example, bookshops such as Waterstone's are selling increasing volumes of books using the internet. This has profound implications for workforce planning, as different numbers of employees may be needed for the internet operation, in different locations and with different skills.
- **Human capital.** A business that has appropriately skilled employees who are well rewarded and highly motivated are an asset to the organisation and may offer it a competitive advantage. To make such employees redundant (or to redeploy them) because of a forecast decline in sales may not make sense if this proves to be a short-term decline, or does not occur at all. Retaining human capital in the business will be a priority for many managers, irrespective of short-term changes in demand.
- **Migration.** In the early years of the twenty-first century, large numbers of economic migrants came from eastern Europe to the UK. This gave UK businesses access to a substantial source of relatively cheap labour. This may have contributed to keeping wage rates down in certain low- to medium-skill occupations, and have persuaded HR managers to use labour rather than technology in the production process.
- **Global markets.** A large number of businesses trade in global markets and thus may use employees drawn from many countries and cultures. This can assist workforce planning by accessing a wide range of skills, but make it more difficult by increasing communication problems.

2.4 The value of workforce planning

Workforce planning offers real benefits to businesses. It enables managers to have the right employees available in the right place with the right skills. This gives the business a greater chance of meeting the needs of its customers and winning repeat orders. For businesses supplying services, a well-trained workforce can provide a competitive advantage and allow more flexibility in pricing decisions. Managing people effectively is a common feature of successful organisations and this become easier if changes are planned in advance and implemented following an agreed process. This is impossible without planning.

Planning in any function within a business encourages managers to look forward, to assess likely changes and to prepare considered responses. HR is no different from any other function in the business.

There are circumstances where workforce planning is more difficult and where it might be of less value. Businesses operating in markets that are subject to wide fluctuations in costs and demand might experience problems in assessing the volume and value of products that they expect to sell and therefore in assessing the quantity and types of labour that they require. The value of workforce planning depends to a significant extent on the accuracy of forecasts of revenues and costs.

3 Competitive organisational structures

What you need to know:
- the organisational structures available to businesses
- factors determining the choice of organisational structure
- methods of adapting organisational structures to improve competitiveness

3.1 The organisational structures available to businesses

Businesses can organise themselves internally in a number of ways. The two main organisational structures they may use are:
- functional
- matrix

Functional structures

An organisational structure that is functional is illustrated in Figure 5.2.

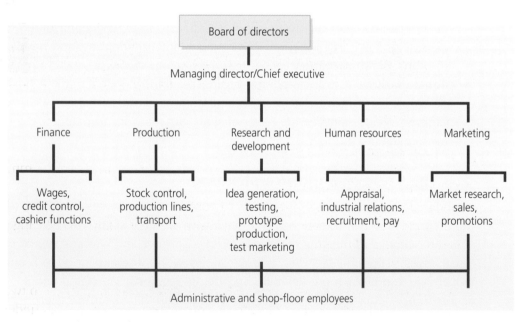

Figure 5.2 *A functional structure*

The advantages of a functional structure are:
- It allows the business to be coordinated from the top and to have a sense of overall direction.
- It provides clear lines of communication and authority for all employees.
- It lets specialists operate in particular areas, such as marketing and research and development, and to develop new and innovative ideas.

Equally, there are disadvantages of a functional structure:
* Senior managers may become remote as the business grows and may become unaware of local issues.
* Decision making may be slow because of long lines of communication, which may damage competitiveness.
* It provides little coordination and direction to those lower in the organisation.

Matrix structures

The matrix structure (see Figure 5.3) was first used in the USA and has become more popular in the UK. This type of structure combines the traditional departments seen in Figure 5.2 with project teams. For example, a project or task team established to develop a new product might include engineers and design specialists as well as those with marketing, financial, HR and production skills. These teams can be temporary or permanent depending on the tasks they are asked to complete. Each team member can end up with two or more line managers — their normal departmental manager as well as the manager of the project.

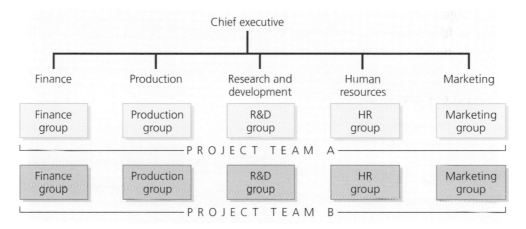

Figure 5.3 A matrix structure

The advantages of a matrix structure are:
* It can help to break down traditional department barriers, improving communication across the entire organisation.
* It can allow individuals to use particular skills in a variety of contexts.
* It avoids the need for several departments to meet regularly, so reducing costs and improving coordination.

The disadvantages are:
* Members of project teams may have divided loyalties, as they report to two or more line managers. Equally, this scenario can put project team members under a heavy pressure of work.
* There may not be a clear line of accountability for project teams, given the complex nature of matrix structures.

Other organisational structures

Two other organisational structures are sometimes used:
* **Entrepreneurial structures** are frequently found in small businesses operating in competitive markets. A few key workers at the core of the organisation — often the owner(s) — make decisions. The business is heavily dependent on the knowledge and skills of these key workers.

- **Informal structures** exist where the organisation does not have an obvious structure. This is common is the case of professionals (e.g. doctors and lawyers), where they operate as a team. The professionals normally receive administrative support from others within the organisation.

3.2 Factors determining the choice of organisational structure

When deciding upon an organisational structure, a business will take into account several factors:

- **The environment in which the business is operating.** Fierce competitive pressures may encourage delayering (see opposite) in an effort to reduce costs, while rapid change can emphasise the need for a matrix structure to ensure that the organisation remains up to date. The matrix structure would also eliminate the possibility of inflexible hierarchies getting in the way of rapid decision making.
- **The size of the business.** Many small businesses begin with an entrepreneurial structure, with the owner playing a central role. He or she will not be able to sustain this position as the business grows and a large firm is more likely be organised traditionally, or perhaps as a matrix.
- **The corporate objectives of the business.** An innovative and highly competitive organisation may opt for a matrix structure in order to complete tasks effectively. On the other hand, a business focusing on quality of design and production (as opposed to growth) may suit an entrepreneurial structure. The latter structure may also be appropriate for businesses in a craft industry.
- **The skills of the workforce.** The higher the level of skill that the typical employee has, the more likely it is that businesses will organise along matrix or informal lines. A small group of professionals, such as management consultants or estate agents, may simply carry out their professional duties with administrative support from the organisation. Less skilled employees may respond better to a more formal structure, with more authority retained further up the hierarchy.
- **The culture of the organisation.** If a business has a highly innovative culture, wishing to be a market leader selling advanced products, it may adopt a matrix structure to minimise bureaucracy and to allow teams to carry out the necessary research and development and market research. On the other hand, an organisation that values tradition (and derives its commercial success from appearing conventional) may be best suited to a formal hierarchical structure. This structure places emphasis on positions rather than people and encourages the continuance of existing policies. Some high-class hotels fall into this category.

Examiner's tip

Think about the type of product and the competitiveness and nature of the market in which it is sold when tackling questions on organisational structures. For example, a firm operating in a rapidly changing market such as computer software might benefit from using a matrix structure.

3.3 Methods of adapting organisational structures to improve competitiveness

Managers can use a number of means of adapting their organisational structures to improve the competitiveness of their businesses.

Delayering

Many businesses in the manufacturing and service sectors have moved towards flatter organisational structures through **delayering**. Delayering involves removing one or more levels of hierarchy from the organisational structure. This idea crossed the Atlantic from the USA.

Frequently, the layers removed are those containing middle managers. For example, many high-street banks no longer have a manager in each of their branches, preferring to appoint a manager to oversee a number of branches.

There are a number of advantages of delayering an organisational structure:
- It offers opportunities for delegation, empowerment and motivation, as the number of managers is reduced and more authority is given to shop-floor workers.
- It can improve communication within the organisation, as messages have to pass through fewer levels of hierarchy.
- It can remove departmental rivalry if department heads are removed and the workforce is organised in teams.
- It can reduce costs, as fewer employees are required and employing middle managers can be expensive.

As with all management techniques, however, delayering has some potential disadvantages:
- Not all organisations are suited to flatter organisational structures — mass production industries with low-skilled employees may not adapt easily.
- Delayering can have a negative impact on motivation due to job losses, especially if it is really just an excuse for redundancies and cost-cutting.
- Initial disruption may occur as people take on new responsibilities and fulfil new roles.
- Those managers remaining will have a wider span of control, which, if it is too wide, can damage communication within the business.

The use of flexible workforces

Flexible workforces are those that are adaptable to changing conditions and demands. A flexible workforce is likely to be multiskilled, well trained and not resistant to change. Performance-related pay may be used to encourage labour flexibility.

Flexible workforces can take a number of forms:
- Some of the workforce may be on **part-time and temporary contracts**, allowing the business to adapt smoothly to changes in the level of demand for its products.
- Employees may be on **fixed short-term contracts**. This is beneficial in that workers are not employed any longer than necessary, and expensive redundancy payments can be avoided. However, such contracts may have a negative impact upon the motivation and performance of employees.
- Employees may work **flexible hours** through either flexitime or an annualised hours system. The former entails employees having to be at work during 'core hours' each day (maybe 10 a.m. until 4 p.m.) and making up the balance of hours at times that suit them. The latter system allows employers to ask staff to work longer hours during busy periods, with time taken in lieu during quieter periods.

- Employees may be required to work from a number of locations. Alternatively, they may be required to **telework** — to work from home, using computers and other technology to communicate with colleagues and customers.
- **Multiskilled employees** are an important element of a flexible workforce. Their ability to switch from one job to another as demand changes, or when colleagues are absent, allows a business to meet the demands of the market more easily and responsively.

The advantages and disadvantages of flexible workforces are outlined in Table 5.2.

Advantages	Disadvantages
<ul><li>Firms can more easily meet fluctuations in demand.</li><li>It is simpler to cover for absent staff.</li><li>Wage costs may be reduced.</li><li>Firms can meet the demand for highly specialised skills relatively cheaply.</li><li>Firms can respond rapidly to changing circumstances.</li></ul>	<ul><li>Communication problems may occur if employees are used irregularly.</li><li>Systems such as empowerment and team working may prove difficult to implement.</li><li>Lack of security may detract from employee motivation and morale.</li><li>A higher turnover of labour may result.</li></ul>

Table 5.2 The advantages and disadvantages of flexible workforces

Examiner's tip

Labour forces are an important determinant of competitiveness. Many firms have invested a lot of time, energy and training in making their employees more flexible and better able to cope with rapidly changing environments. However, there are disadvantages of flexibility, and some industries are not particularly suited to this type of labour force (e.g. those requiring low-skilled employees). This is a popular area for questions, and one on which you should relate the theory carefully to the circumstances of the question.

Delegation

Delegation can be defined as the passing of authority to a subordinate within the organisation. Although a task may be passed down from a superior to a subordinate, the manager still has responsibility for making sure that the job is completed. It is possible to delegate authority (i.e. the power to carry out the task), but responsibility remains with the delegator.

To delegate, a manager must trust the delegatee and it is important that the subordinate feels that trust is placed in him or her. A prudent manager will also want to exercise some control over the subordinate — for example, via reports and inspections. Any increase in control exercised by the manager decreases the amount of trust enjoyed by the subordinate. The use of delegation has implications for the workloads of both parties involved.

The advantages and disadvantages of delegation are outlined in Table 5.3.

Advantages	Disadvantages
● Delegation and trust are cheap — they free seniors for other (strategic) matters.	● Trusting subordinates can be risky and responsibility remains with the senior.
● Delegation may also breed a sense of responsibility.	● Controlling subordinates is safe in that abuse is avoided.
● Controlling subordinates is expensive.	● Delegation requires (expensive) training for subordinates.
● Delegation allows specialisation.	● Once trust is given, it is impossible to withdraw it without loss of face.
● Delegation allows individuals to develop skills and careers.	● Trust is fragile: once broken, it is never the same.
● Without delegation there is no training for prospective managers.	
● Too little delegation leads to senior managers overworking.	

Table 5.3 Delegation — the balance sheet

Centralisation and decentralisation

Centralisation occurs when the majority of decisions are the responsibility of just a few people at the top of the organisation. In many senses, centralisation is the opposite of delegation.

Decentralisation occurs when control shifts sideways or horizontally (between people at the same level in the organisation), while delegation implies a downward shift in control. Decentralisation is not the same as delegation but is often accompanied by it.

Decentralisation offers a range of benefits in terms of offering employees the prospect of greater independence in their working lives, known as **empowerment**, and the motivational benefits that can result from this. Disadvantages of decentralisation are the training costs that might be incurred and the possible loss of a common sense of direction throughout the organisation.

Examiner's tip

Delegation is an important element in many examination answers, particularly those requiring analysis and evaluation. It may be a key component of arguments relating to implementation of team working, empowerment, etc. It is important to recognise that this approach has advantages and disadvantages, and a well-balanced answer will reflect this. This can be an important part of developing an analytical line of argument.

4 *Effective employer–employee relations*

What you need to know:
● how employers manage communications with employees
● methods of employee representation
● methods of avoiding and resolving industrial disputes

4.1 How employers manage communications with employees

Communication is the exchange of information between people within and outside organisations. Effective communication systems are important to all businesses. Often, communication is not given the attention it deserves and many managers underestimate its role within a successful organisation. In particular, effective communication can help to maintain good relations between employers and employees.

Employers are likely to use a number of techniques to communicate with employees, including the following:

- **Meetings.** These can occur in a variety of forms, including formal meetings with trade unions or other groups representing employees, and less formal discussions between individual representatives of the two sides. Social events may also provide forums for the exchange of information.
- **Presentations.** These are frequently used in businesses to explain policies and procedures to large groups of employees. Many presentations use Microsoft PowerPoint®. Detailed information (especially relating to employment and working practices) can be exchanged using this software.
- **Electronic mail (e-mail).** This method of communication allows computers to speak to one another throughout the world for the cost of a local telephone call. Messages are stored on servers and can be accessed by the recipient through the use of a password. This is particularly useful for quick international communication between employers' and employees' groups across different time zones, as messages can be stored until the recipient is available.
- **Intranets.** These are electronic, computer-based communication networks, similar to the internet but used internally by individual businesses. They are ideally suited to large companies, especially those with a number of locations. They provide an e-mail service as well as access to information of interest to large numbers of employees.
- **Video conferencing.** This allows people to communicate face to face while in different locations, nationally or internationally. It saves time and avoids the need for employers and employees to travel to meetings.

Communication can play an important part in motivating the workforce. Encouraging (and listening to) the views and opinions of all employees, perhaps through feedback, will increase their sense of self-worth and should improve motivation. It may also be the source of some good ideas — for example, through quality circles. Such upward communication is a central element in team work and empowerment.

Effective internal communication can help to provide greater understanding of differences in cultures and opinions within an organisation. Employees may take a different perspective on the business and its activities from those of managers. It is likely that as stakeholders the two groups have different aims. Effective methods of communication will help the two parties to understand each other's viewpoints and may reduce the number of misunderstandings and the possibility of disputes.

4.2 Methods of employee representation

Trade unions

A **trade union** is an organised group of employees, which aims to protect and enhance the economic position of its members. Trade unions offer a number of advantages to their members:

- negotiation of pay and conditions on behalf of their members, including hours worked and holidays
- protection from unsafe working practices
- improved job security
- a range of associated services, including financial and legal advice

When trade unions negotiate with employers on behalf of their members on matters such as pay, conditions and fringe benefits, this is called **collective bargaining**. They are usually in a better position to negotiate than individuals because they have more negotiating skills and power.

In contrast, **individual bargaining** involves each individual employee negotiating his or her own pay and working conditions. Individual bargaining occurs when no union exists or when confident and/or talented individuals feel they will negotiate better terms on their own.

Employers can also benefit from the existence of trade unions for the following reasons:
- They act as a communications link between management and employees.
- Professional negotiation on behalf of a large number of employees can save time and reduce the likelihood of disputes occurring.

In addition to the above functions, trade unions negotiate grievance and disciplinary procedures, and job descriptions and job specifications.

The changing role of trade unions in the UK

Union membership rose from the 1950s until the mid-1970s. Since then it has fallen steadily, although since 2000 there have been signs of a revival in union membership. The decline has occurred for a number of reasons:

- **Legislation to control the activities of unions.** The Conservative governments of the 1980s and early 1990s passed a series of acts to limit the impact of unions on business activities. In particular, this legislation made secret ballots on disputes mandatory and restricted the number of pickets.
- **The decline of traditional industries.** The shipbuilding and steel industries were strongly unionised. The fact that these industries have declined and employ far fewer people means that the unions associated with them have also become less important.
- **The increasing number of small businesses.** There has been a rise in the number of small businesses in the UK since the 1980s. These firms are not strongly unionised because they employ few people (and many are part time) and relationships are such that a union is often considered unnecessary.
- **The changing composition of the UK's workforce.** More employees are now female and part time than previously, and they are less likely to be members of unions. Simultaneously, fewer young employees have entered the workforce because of falling birth rates, so unions have had fewer potential recruits.

Other factors, apart from declining membership, have contributed to the declining influence of unions in the UK economy:

- **Single union agreements.** These agreements have been more common since the late 1980s. Under such agreements, employees agree to be represented by one union. This makes negotiation simpler for the employers (as there are only two parties to the discussions) while reducing the possibility of disputes between rival unions. They also assist in developing single status within the organisation and eliminating differences between blue-collar and white-collar workers. Finally, they help maintain good communications between employers and employees, lessening the possibility of expensive and damaging industrial action.

- **No-strike deals.** This type of agreement originated in Japan and is most common among Japanese firms in the UK. While these deals have made the UK a more attractive location for international investment, they have altered the balance of power in favour of the employer. However, British unions have tended to sign them only when binding arbitration is a part of the deal. This means that, in the event of a dispute, an independent third party can impose a settlement.

- **Union derecognition.** Some businesses do not recognise unions in the workplace. Although in certain cases this has been a means of achieving a single union position, in others the aim has been to eliminate unions from the workplace entirely. This process has frequently been accompanied by financial inducements to the workforce. However, the Employment Relations Act (2000) has reversed this trend to some extent, as it grants unions the right to recognition as long as they have over 50% of the workforce as members.

Other methods of representation

There are other ways in which employees' views can be represented within the business. **Industrial democracy** gives employees the means of influencing the decision-making processes and of representing their views to employers. Some businesses genuinely attempt to involve employees in decision making, while others implement relevant methods to improve public relations internally and externally.

The main methods of promoting industrial democracy are as follows:

- **Worker directors.** These are shop-floor representatives who are (usually) elected to be members of the board of directors of a business. Worker directors were advocated by the Bullock Report in 1977. Unions sometimes oppose the appointment of such directors because other workers may see them as having a hand in implementing unpopular policies, so blurring the distinction between employers and employees. Managers sometimes fear that worker directors may leak sensitive financial information. In recent years, the EU has encouraged the appointment of worker directors.

- **Works councils.** These provides a basis for regular meetings between representatives from management and employees. Works councils focus on ideas to improve the performance of the organisation at all levels. Negotiations on pay and conditions are left to other forums.

4.3 Methods of avoiding and resolving industrial disputes

In most cases, disputes can be resolved without trade unions or other employee groups being forced into industrial action. The improvement in industrial relations in recent years has, in part, been a consequence of two main techniques.

Arbitration

Arbitration resolves a dispute by appointing an independent person or panel to decide on a way of settling the dispute. It can take several forms:

- **Non-binding arbitration** involves a neutral third party making an award to settle a dispute that the parties concerned can accept or not.
- **Binding arbitration** means that parties to the dispute have to take the award of the arbitrator.
- **Pendulum arbitration** means that the decision is binding and the arbitrator has to decide entirely for one side or the other. 'Splitting the difference' is not an option. This system avoids excessive claims by unions and miserly offers by employers.

Conciliation

Conciliation is a method of resolving individual or collective disputes in which a neutral third party encourages the continuation of negotiation rather than industrial action. The conciliator's role does not involve making any judgement concerning the validity of the position of either party.

Advisory, Conciliation and Arbitration Service

The Advisory, Conciliation and Arbitration Service (ACAS) was set up in 1975 as an independent body with the responsibility to prevent or resolve industrial disputes. ACAS is financed by the government and originated during a period of severe industrial action in the 1970s when both employers and employees called for a mechanism for resolving disputes.

ACAS provides employers and employees with arbitration and conciliation services. The organisation also offers other services:

- It advises employers, trade unions and employers' associations on topics such as reducing absenteeism, employee sickness and payment systems.
- It investigates individual cases of discrimination and unfair dismissal.
- It focuses on improving business practices to reduce the possibility of industrial disputes.

1 General advice in preparing for Unit 3

1.1 The examination

Key facts relating to this examination are set out below:

- Duration: 1 hour and 45 minutes.
- A decision-making case study with several appendices of data.
- Approximately four questions.
- The final question will have an allocation of more than 30 marks.
- Most papers will require you to complete a calculation.
- Total marks available: 80.
- Available: January and June from January 2010.

This unit looks at functional strategies. The examination will require you to tackle a number of questions, including a major final one. The earlier questions will look at different functional aspects of the business's activities and are likely to ask you to complete a calculation. The final question will ask you either to assess a strategy that a business is proposing or has implemented, or to devise and justify a functional strategy appropriate to the circumstances.

Besides completing a calculation, this examination paper will require you to interpret data (set out in the appendices) as well as the case study itself. This skill will be particularly important in tackling the final (high-mark) question. Performing well on this final question is essential for anyone who is aiming to achieve an A* grade for the whole A-level qualification.

A copy of AQA's specimen Unit 3 paper and the marking scheme can be found at:

www.aqa.org.uk/qual/gce/pdf/business_studies_new.php

1.2 How to prepare for the Unit 3 examination

This examination requires you to have mastered all of the material that comprises Unit 3 and there is quite a lot of it — knowledge is therefore essential. The questions on this paper will be fairly broad and offer you some choice as to what material to concentrate on. This is especially true of the final, high-mark question. You will have a large number of possible arguments that you can offer in response to this question. However, selecting the most important and relevant ones will be a vital element in succeeding in the examination. You should seek to develop a small number of arguments as fully as possible, and to use the material in the case and the data in the appendices to apply your arguments and support your judgements.

Your revision should seek to explore the links that exist between the relevant functions of the business. For example, you should consider how implementing a particular financial strategy might impact on the other functions of the business. Understanding and analysing the inter-functional links within the case study will assist you in writing a high-quality response.

However, this examination also tests the skills of application, analysis and evaluation. As shown in Table 6.1, they carry 80% of the marks on this paper.

Skill	Marks	%
Knowledge	16	20
Application	24	30
Analysis	20	25
Evaluation	20	25
Total	80	100

Table 6.1 Mark allocations for Unit 3

Application

Application is the skill of applying your answers to the context set out in the examination paper. This is an important skill in Unit 3. Each of the Unit 3 case studies will provide you with information about a particular business and a fair proportion of this information is likely to be in the form of numbers. It is essential that you relate your answers to this business and avoid writing general theoretical answers. The examiner will include hooks for you to use in developing your responses — these may be numerical in form. He or she may say that the business faces rising unit costs, is aiming to decentralise or suffers from high levels of gearing. These are things that you can use in your answers to help to gain application marks.

Analysis

Analysis is developing a line of argument and following it through. This skill carries 25% of marks on this paper. Analysis commonly focuses on causes or effects or on interrelationships. Do think about the theories that you have studied in this unit and consider how they can be used to help businesses to improve their performance. You will remember from answering AS questions that those requiring analysis use verbs (or command words) such as 'analyse' and 'examine'.

Evaluation

Evaluation is the skill of judgement. Most questions on Unit 3 will require evaluation and the proportion of marks awarded for this skill is relatively high. You should remember that you can recognise evaluative questions by the command words that are used. Evaluative questions use the following words or phrases: 'discuss', 'assess', 'consider', 'evaluate', 'to what extent' and 'justify'.

Good evaluation on Unit 3 will depend on mastery of the skill of application by making judgements about this specific business, rather than businesses in general. So you must spend sufficient time reading the case study carefully and pondering the data set out in the appendices. You should think what is significant about the business scenario set out in the case study. Think about the case study at three levels:

- **The market in which the business is trading.** You should consider matters such as: is it highly competitive, and on what basis do firms compete? Is it growing or shrinking?
- **The business itself.** Think about the four functional areas of the business. How do they interrelate and is one function relatively weak or strong?
- **The product that the business sells.** Is the product price elastic and what is the length of its life cycle? Does it have a USP or a strong brand image?

These ideas are only guides and the list is not comprehensive. It is important for you to think in depth about the business scenario with which you have been presented.

You should also look carefully at the appendices and assess what they tell you about the business. Note the following:

- Are the data historical or forecast?
- What do they tell you about the various functions of the business?
- Does it support the story told in the case (and perhaps the expectations of the business's managers)?
- Are there any links between the appendices that will allow you to develop stronger and more effective lines of analysis?

You should be prepared to spend up to 15 minutes reading the case study and appendices. This might seem an unproductive period in a time-constrained examination, but is an essential part of tackling this examination paper successfully.

Remember that good evaluation makes a clear judgement and supports it.

2 | A sample Unit 3 examination paper

Stellar Transport plc

Stellar Transport plc's board of directors faced a major decision. The company is one of the UK's best-known transport businesses with interests in coach, lorry and air transport both in the UK and in other countries, such as the USA, Canada, most EU countries, Israel and South Africa. The company had expanded steadily throughout the 1990s and the early years of the twenty-first century to become one of the UK's largest businesses.

The company's tough chief executive, Tom Ellard, had led the business throughout this period and has been uncompromising in his pursuit of profits. He argued that the company's shareholders are the most important stakeholder group and deserve the best possible returns on their investments. Because of this, he sought to minimise costs wherever possible, even though this caused disputes with groups of workers in the UK and overseas. The company's successful growth was based on the operation of a low-cost, low-price strategy in the various transport markets in which it operated.

Until a few years ago, Stellar Transport was a star performer on the Stock Exchange, offering investors excellent returns and promising further growth in the years ahead. Since then the company's financial performances have been less impressive. A number of factors have been responsible for the change in fortune. The company's decision to invest heavily in operating a business-class airline service across the Atlantic was judged by many analysts to be a poor decision. The downturn in the world economy in 2008 seemed to justify this view. At the same time, a number of industrial disputes within the company proved damaging to its performance and to its reputation. Tom Ellard retained considerable control over decision making throughout the business, despite its increasing size. Some employees resented the lack of empowerment and believed that decisions made at the centre were often made without full understanding of the particular conditions prevailing in the local markets.

The decline in the company's performance led to pressure for change throughout the business. At a board level there was considerable discussion about the way in which the

business managed its employees. Some directors felt that a policy of empowerment was essential, but Tom Ellard defended his approach to managing employees successfully. He did, however, acknowledge the need for a review of the company's traditional and highly centralised organisational structure and conceded that changes were needed to the structure to improve the competitiveness of the business.

The directors also expressed concerns about the direction of the company's marketing. Their concerns were twofold. Firstly, they argued that there was often a lack of detailed market analysis before major decisions were taken and this had recently resulted in a number of unprofitable ventures. There was also a lack of a clear marketing strategy. The company appeared to take different approaches in different markets and had moved away from its successful low-cost strategy over the last few years.

Stellar Transport plc's board of directors were faced with a major decision. In a scenario of declining profits, the directors were keen to turn things around and favoured further expansion as a means of generating new sources of income and profits. Two options lay before them and they had to choose one, as the company could not raise sufficient finance to invest in both.

Option 1

The company could bid to operate a newly available rail franchise in the south of England. This would require it to pay a substantial fee to the UK government for the right to run services on these lines and to invest in new trains and carriages to supply the services. The company had not operated a rail franchise in the past but believed that it could provide these services, many of which were used by commuters working in London. The project could be administered from Stellar Transport's head offices in London.

Option 2

This required a larger investment in buying a low-cost airline that provides flights between major cities in five countries in south Asia, including China. The business has enjoyed rising revenues and profits using the low-cost model employed by airlines in the UK such as easyJet. The market in Asia for air travel is growing, although new competitors are appearing. Stellar Transport plc has not operated any transport systems in Asia before.

Appendix A: Forecast net cash flows for the two alternative investments

Year	Rail project Net cash flows (£m)	Air Asia Net cash flows (£m)
2009	(120)	(250)
2010	35	90
2011	50	95
2012	53	110
2013	54	150

Appendix B: Accounts for Stellar Transport plc (year to March 2009)

Income statement (profit and loss account) Year to 31 March 2009		Balance sheet As at 31 March 2009	
	£m		£m
Turnover	**402.6**	**Non-current assets**	**606.4**
Cost of sales	163.4	Stock	24.7
Gross profit	**239.2**	Debtors	23.3
Overheads	135.7	Cash	23.9
Depreciation	11.2	Payables (creditors)	78.1
Operating profit	**92.3**	**Net current assets**	**(6.2)**
One-off item	5.9	Non-current liabilities	(296.6)
Pre-tax profit	**86.4**	**Net assets employed**	**303.6**
		Share capital	194.5
		Reserves	109.1
		Capital employed	**600.2**

Appendix C: Key marketing data

Item	Rail project	Air Asia
Estimated price elasticity of demand for the product	−0.25	−1.88
Forecast average annual growth in consumer expenditure, 2010–15	11%	24%
Number of direct competitors	0	4
Proposed average annual marketing budget (£000s)	145,000	575,000

Appendix D: Other data

Item	Rail project	Air Asia
Estimated impact of decision on company's annual fixed costs	+£1.8 million	+£19 .6 million
Number of new office locations required	0	9
Number of additional employees required	460	1,250
Percentage of additional workforce belonging to a recognised trade union	74%	2%
Number of languages spoken by additional employees	1	7

Questions

1 Use relevant investment appraisal techniques to compare the financial returns of the two expansion projects. (10 marks)

2 Stellar Transport plc intends to adapt its organisational structure to improve the competitiveness of the business. Discuss the possible methods it might use to achieve this objective. (18 marks)

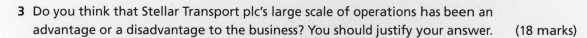

3 Do you think that Stellar Transport plc's large scale of operations has been an advantage or a disadvantage to the business? You should justify your answer.   (18 marks)

4 Using all the information available to you, complete the following tasks:

   (a) analyse the case for Stellar Transport plc choosing option 1

   (b) analyse the case for Stellar Transport plc choosing option 2

   (c) make a justified recommendation on which option the company should choose   (34 marks)

Total marks: 80

Unit 4
The business environment and managing change

1 Understanding mission, aims and objectives

What you need to know:
- mission statements
- corporate aims and objectives
- corporate strategies
- different stakeholder perspectives

The term 'corporate' refers to the entire business. Until now we have been considering individual functions of the business, such as marketing and human resources. From this point on, we shall look at the entire organisation.

1.1 Mission statements

Mission statements summarise a business's long-term aims and are intended to provide the organisation with a sense of common purpose. Organisations attempt to encapsulate the purpose of their existence in a single sentence, which represents its vision or mission. Coca-Cola says that its mission is to 'get more people to drink Coke than water'. This reflects its mission to dominate the market.

Mission statements focus on:
- corporate values
- non-financial objectives
- benefits of the business to the community
- how consumers are to be satisfied

Figure 7.1 shows the hierarchy of objectives stemming from a mission statement.

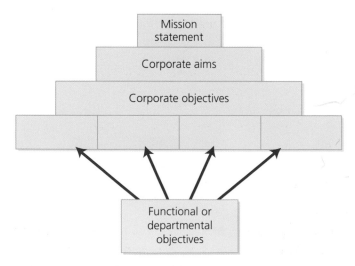

Figure 7.1 The hierarchy of objectives

1.2 Corporate aims and objectives

Corporate aims

Corporate aims are long-term plans from which company objectives are derived. They do not normally state targets in numerical terms. From these aims or mission statements, a company can set quantifiable objectives, such as gaining market leadership in Europe within 3 years.

Corporate objectives

Corporate objectives are medium- to long-term goals established to coordinate the business. Objectives should be quantified and have a stated timescale, such as to earn a 20% return on capital next year. Businesses may have a number of objectives.

Survival

Survival is an important objective:
- during periods of recession or intense competition
- at a time of crisis, such as during a hostile takeover bid

Profit maximisation

Profits are maximised when the difference between sales revenue and total costs is at its greatest. Some firms seek to earn the greatest possible profits to satisfy their shareholders' desire for high dividends. Others are content to pursue a satisfactory level of profit. Known as **satisficing**, this is common among small firms where higher profits may require the entrepreneur to work excessive hours.

Growth

Many businesses pursue growth because their managers believe that the organisation will not survive otherwise. If a firm grows, it should be able to exploit its market position and earn higher profits. This benefits shareholders (in the long term) by providing greater dividends as well as offering better salaries and more job security to the employees and managers of the business.

Managerial objectives

Managers can pursue their own objectives rather than those set by the owners (shareholders). Managerial objectives might include:
- maximising leisure time
- maximising financial rewards — pension, bonuses and salary
- seeking to take over rival companies
- establishing modern working practices
- improving professional status

Corporate image

This has become a more important objective for many companies recently. Companies fear that consumers who have a negative view of them will not purchase their products. This applies to any action that damages the company image.

Which objectives should be pursued?

The objectives pursued by a business vary according to its size, ownership and legal structure. For example, survival might be important to a company during a severe recession, profits to a large public limited company and satisficing to a family-owned private limited company.

A business's objectives can be divided into primary and secondary objectives:

- **Primary objectives** are those which must be achieved if the business is to survive and be successful. These normally relate to issues such as profit levels and market share.
- **Secondary objectives** tend to measure the efficiency of the organisation. They may affect the chances of success, but only in the long term. Examples are customer care, administrative efficiency and labour turnover rates.

Over recent years, customer care has assumed greater importance in many businesses. This means that improvements in this area have been reclassified as a primary objective.

1.3 Corporate strategies

A **corporate strategy** is the medium- to long-term plan by which a business intends to achieve its corporate objectives. The corporate strategy should include:

- the corporate objectives that are being pursued
- the financial resources to be used
- the human resource implications of the plan
- the operational resources that will be required to fulfil the plan

If a business has an objective of profit maximisation, it might employ a strategy of innovation or of growth by merger and takeover. The objective can be viewed as the destination for the firm; the strategy is the means to get to the destination.

1.4 Different stakeholder perspectives

Stakeholders are any individuals or groups with an interest in a particular organisation. Stakeholders include:

- managers
- shareholders
- employees
- consumers
- local residents
- creditors
- suppliers

Some of the objectives of stakeholders are common; others are unique to particular types of stakeholder. This is illustrated in Table 7.1.

Some objectives may be supported by a number of stakeholders, whereas others can be more controversial. For example:

- A **positive corporate image** would be a fairly uncontroversial objective among stakeholders. Most interested parties would benefit from a business pursuing such an objective.
- **Maximum short-term profits** might be popular with shareholders, but consumers would oppose this because it might mean high prices, and employees might object because it might mean wages are held down.
- **Social responsibility** involves considering all of society's needs when taking decisions, such as limiting night-time working or building on more expensive brownfield sites as opposed to unused greenfield sites. These decisions may be well received by local residents and employees, but shareholders could be upset by reductions in profits and dividends.

Stakeholder	Likely objectives
Employees	• Job security • High wages • Good working conditions
Shareholders	• Maximum short-term profits • Long-term growth • Positive corporate image
Local residents	• Minimal pollution • Maximum employment • Job security
Suppliers	• Prompt payment • Regular orders • Growth (increasing scale of orders)
Consumers	• High-quality products • Innovative products • Low prices

Table 7.1 Stakeholder objectives

Nowadays, there is much more interest in the idea that firms should fulfil their social responsibilities. Businesses have to consider their actions in the context of a wide range of groups and not just their shareholders.

A number of issues arise from the study of stakeholders and their different perspectives:
- Companies may claim to care about all their stakeholders for purely public relations reasons.
- Even firms that genuinely wish to meet the needs of all stakeholders may find many managers stuck in the previous culture. The change to a stakeholder culture can take years.
- The stakeholder approach can lead to many benefits for organisations, such as winning new customers and attracting high-quality employees.

The stakeholder approach may prove to be just a fad. When the profits of firms fall, for example, they may decide that short-term profit is much more important than obligations to other groups.

Examiner's tip

It is important to be aware that, while stakeholders' objectives can coincide, they can also be the basis of conflict. For example, local residents, trade unions, shareholders and most other stakeholders would support the objective of improving a business's corporate image. Disagreement might occur, however, if the business had to spend substantial sums of money in the process.

8 Assessing changes in the business environment

At this point in the development of our 'story' we examine the impact on the business of various external causes of change. Unit 4 requires you to assess the likely impact of these changes and to consider how businesses might respond to them.

1 The relationship between businesses and the economic environment

What you need to know:
- the impact of economic factors
- trends in key economic variables
- the globalisation of markets
- developments in emerging markets
- the responses of businesses to changes in the economic environment

This topic also requires you to evaluate the strategies that businesses might deploy in response to these changes. We will consider a range of strategies at the end of this section.

Examiner's tip

You should relate the theory we cover in Unit 4 to a diverse range of large businesses. It is important for you to see how different businesses respond to similar changes in the economic environment.

1.1 The impact of economic factors

The level of economic activity

This refers to the amount of production, expenditure and employment in the economy. A central measure of the level of economic activity is the level of **national income** or **gross national product** (GNP).

The level of economic activity is an important factor in assessing the economic environment in which businesses operate (see Table 8.1). The government tries to manipulate the level of economic activity to provide a positive environment for businesses: for example, by attempting to avoid severe booms and slumps in the trade cycle.

Indicators of rising levels of economic activity	Indicators of falling levels of economic activity
• Increasing output	• Declining levels of production
• Rising expenditure by consumers and businesses	• Falling expenditure by consumers and businesses
• Increasing tax revenue	• Declining tax revenue
• Increasing purchases of imports	• Possible decline in imports
• Greater levels of employment	• Rising unemployment levels
• Build-up of inflationary pressure	• Economic growth slowing and possibly negative
• Economic growth sustained and perhaps increasing	• Possible increase in saving

Table 8.1 Indicators of rising and falling levels of economic activity

A number of means are available to the government to alter the level of economic activity in the economy, as shown in Table 8.2. (Government policies are considered more fully on pages 97–100.)

Actions to increase the level of economic activity	Actions to reduce the level of economic activity
• Reducing direct taxes, such as income tax	• Increasing rates of direct taxes
• Lowering indirect taxes, such as VAT	• Increasing rates of indirect taxes
• Increasing government expenditure	• Reducing government expenditure
• Implementing policies designed to encourage export sales	• Implementing policies designed to increase savings
• Reducing interest rates	• Increasing interest rates

Table 8.2 Actions to increase and reduce the level of economic activity

The government manages the economy and alters the level of economic activity in order to achieve a number of objectives. These include:
- steady and sustained economic growth, avoiding the worst booms and slumps associated with the trade cycle
- price stability
- a low rate of unemployment
- a stable exchange rate for the pound sterling

The economic environment for UK businesses is increasingly determined by the actions of the EU. The creation of the single currency (the euro) and the introduction of monetary union reflect the growing importance of Europe. This influence will become greater if the UK decides to adopt the euro.

The trade cycle

The **trade cycle**, also known as the **business cycle**, describes the regular fluctuations in economic activity occurring over time in all economies. Figure 8.1 illustrates the components of a typical trade cycle.

The trade cycle is a major influence on the performance of businesses for two reasons.
- As the economy moves from one stage of the trade cycle to another, businesses can expect to see substantial changes in their trading conditions.
- The government's economic policies are likely to change along with the stage of the trade cycle to compensate for the alteration of the environment in which businesses are operating.

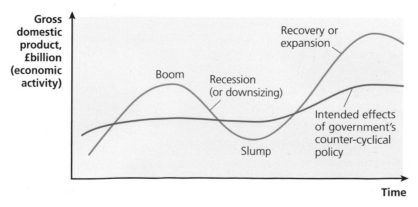

Figure 8.1 The stages of the trade cycle

Figure 8.1 illustrates a smooth and regular trade cycle. In reality, the change in gross domestic product (a measure of national income) is likely to be irregular as economic cycles of different duration and intensity operate simultaneously.

Trade cycles generally have four stages (see Table 8.3):

(1) **Upswing** or **expansion** as the economy recovers from a slump and output and employment rise.

(2) This is followed by a **boom**, with high levels of output and expenditure by firms, consumers and the government.

(3) A **recession** occurs when incomes and output start to fall as demand declines.

(4) A **slump** takes place when output is at its lowest, unemployment is high and increasing numbers of firms go bankrupt.

Stage of the trade cycle	Possible implications for business	Possible responses of businesses to changing trading conditions
Upswing or expansion	<ul><li>Rising incomes and expenditures</li><li>Possible labour shortages, pushing up wages</li><li>Possible rise in output, encouraging expansion</li></ul>	<ul><li>Opportunity to charge higher prices</li><li>Adoption of more technology to replace expensive labour</li><li>Decide to invest in fixed assets</li><li>Operate nearer to full capacity</li></ul>
Boom	<ul><li>Possible rise in inflation</li><li>Bottlenecks in supply of materials and components</li><li>Unable to satisfy levels of demand as consumption rises</li><li>Profits likely to be high</li></ul>	<ul><li>Face increasing pressure to raise prices regularly</li><li>Seek methods to increase output (maybe producing at overseas plants)</li><li>Offer wage rises to avoid threat of industrial action</li><li>Managers plan for falling levels of demand</li></ul>
Recession	<ul><li>Consumers' disposable incomes start to fall</li><li>Demand for many products begins to fall</li><li>Some businesses experience financial problems</li><li>Excess stocks</li></ul>	<ul><li>Begin to emphasise price competitiveness in advertising</li><li>Seek new markets for existing products</li><li>Lay off some workers or ask them to work short time</li><li>Possible reduction in trade credit provided</li></ul>
Slump	<ul><li>Government may initiate counter-cyclical policies, e.g. lower interest rates</li><li>Rise in number of bankruptcies</li><li>Increased frequency of bad debts</li><li>High levels of unemployment</li></ul>	<ul><li>Offer basic products at bargain prices</li><li>Review credit control policies</li><li>Continue to target new markets</li><li>Seek to diversify product range and sell income-inelastic products</li><li>Reduce wage levels</li></ul>

Table 8.3 Businesses and the trade cycle

Not all businesses and products are equally affected by the trade cycle. Firms selling income-elastic products such as antique furniture or foreign holidays are likely to see sales fall as the economy moves into recession. However, retailers of basic foodstuffs and garages selling petrol will remain relatively unaffected.

Inflation

Inflation can be defined as a persistent rise in the general level of prices and a corresponding fall in the value of money. The UK government measures the rate of inflation by using the **consumer price index** (CPI). The CPI shows changes in the price of the average person's shopping basket and is calculated through a weighted average of each month's price changes. The greater the proportion of household income spent on an item, the bigger is the effect of any price change on the overall inflation figure. So, for example, if expenditure on food is given a 15% weighting, rises in food prices will have a substantial impact on the overall index of inflation.

There are a number of factors that may cause inflation. These causes can be split into two broad groups:

- **Demand-pull inflation.** This occurs when demand for a country's goods and services exceeds its ability to supply these products. Consequently, prices rise as a means of limiting demand to match the available supply. This may be caused by a government allowing firms and individuals to have too much money to spend, perhaps as a result of cutting taxes or lowering interest rates.
- **Cost-push inflation.** This occurs when firms face increasing costs due to factors such as rising wages or higher costs of raw materials and components.

Expectations are an important part of inflation. If businesses anticipate rising inflation, they might take appropriate action, such as raising their prices in anticipation of higher charges from their suppliers. This will, of course, itself contribute to inflation.

Inflation can have a number of adverse effects on businesses:

- Many businesses may suffer falling sales in a period of inflation. Consumers might be expected to spend more during inflationary periods, as they will not wish to hold an asset (money) that is falling in value. However, research shows that people save more (perhaps due to uncertainty) and sales for many businesses fall.
- During periods of high inflation, governments or central banks tend to raise interest rates in an attempt to 'cure' the problem. This can lead to a reduction in sales, as consumers are less inclined to borrow money to purchase more expensive items. Sales of new cars might therefore decline, for example.
- It can be difficult to maintain competitiveness (especially international competitiveness) during bouts of inflation. Rising wages and raw material costs may force firms to raise prices or accept lower profit margins. Firms operating in countries with lower rates of inflation may gain an edge in terms of price competitiveness.
- Businesses may experience difficulty in forecasting sales figures and preparing budgets during periods of high inflation.

Some analysts suggest that low and stable rates of inflation may be beneficial. A steady rise in profits can create favourable expectations and encourage investment by businesses. Inflation can also encourage long-term borrowing by businesses as the real value of their repayments declines over time.

Some economies, notably Japan, have experienced **deflation** over recent years. This occurs when prices fall. This can discourage spending and investment in the economy and lead to a reduction in output and prosperity. Firms are discouraged from investing because of the prospect of lower prices for their products, and consumers delay purchases to benefit from lower prices in the future. The Japanese government has experienced great difficulty in stimulating expansion in its economy because of deflation.

For much of the 1990s and the early part of the twenty-first century, many economies have enjoyed low rates of inflation. However, 2008 saw rising inflation rates across the globe, mainly due to cost-push factors.

Examiner's tip

When writing about the impact of inflation and the possible responses of firms, some consideration of price elasticity can prove a valuable line of argument. Firms operating in a market where demand is price inelastic are less likely to be affected by rising prices. They can increase prices to maintain profit margins.

Unemployment

Unemployment exists when those looking for work cannot find jobs. Governments seek to minimise the level of unemployment for a variety of reasons:

- Unemployment is a waste of resources, as people willing to work are kept idle. If 10% of the workforce is unemployed, output is likely to be correspondingly lower.
- Some of the income generated by those in work will need to be diverted to maintain those who are unable to find employment. Those out of work will claim unemployment benefit or may be placed on costly training schemes such as the New Deal.
- Localised unemployment can result in localised poverty as expenditure falls, firms move away or go bankrupt, and the cycle of increased poverty continues.

A number of different types of unemployment exist:

- **Structural unemployment.** This is the result of fundamental changes in the economy. It may occur because machinery replaces workers, as in the case of bank employees, for whom the use of internet banking has reduced employment. It could also be the result of a decline in the demand for the products of an industry, as in the case of the coal industry.
- **Cyclical unemployment.** This arises from the operation of the trade cycle. In the boom stage, this type of unemployment is minimised. At the other extreme, much of the unemployment experienced during a slump will be cyclical. This type of unemployment is a major target of the government's counter-cyclical policy.
- **Regional unemployment.** This reflects the relative prosperity of the regions of the UK. Traditionally, Northern Ireland, Scotland, Wales and the north of England have suffered higher rates of regional unemployment than the Midlands and the south of England. The UK government and EU authorities operate regional policies in an attempt to alleviate unemployment black spots, although regional spending by the UK government has declined in recent years.
- **Frictional employment.** People moving between jobs cause frictional unemployment. Those who leave jobs may not be able to move into new jobs immediately. While they are searching for employment, they are classified as frictionally unemployed.

The relationship between businesses and the economic environment

Rises in unemployment, actual or forecast, have serious implications for businesses, although the precise impact on firms and their likely responses will depend on circumstances. For example:

- Sales might be expected to fall unless the business is able to sell its products in new markets, perhaps overseas.
- If there is a need to reduce output, then rationalisation and redundancies might follow. Firms may close subsidiary plants. These actions are unlikely to enhance the corporate image of the business.
- Firms generally reduce their levels of inventories during a period of high unemployment in an effort to minimise costs. This can add to the need to reduce current output.
- Research and development plans may be abandoned or postponed, as current levels of demand do not generate enough revenue to finance R&D expenditure.
- The predicted fall in the level of demand may encourage the firm to diversify, particularly into goods and services less susceptible to fluctuations in income. Businesses may consider mergers with other firms to help reduce costs or to broaden product ranges.

If unemployment falls, the effects are reversed.

The precise policies adopted by a firm when faced with changes in unemployment levels might depend on factors such as:

- the organisation's size, financial resources and product range
- the sensitivity of the business's products to changes in income levels — that is, their income elasticity
- the ability of the management team and its responses to changing circumstances

Interest rates

The **rate of interest** can be described as the price of borrowed money. Although we tend to talk of *the* interest rate, there are in fact a range of interest rates operating at any one time. Since May 1997, the Bank of England has had responsibility for setting interest rates. The Bank of England's Monetary Policy Committee (MPC) meets each month and takes decisions on whether to alter interest rates. All other interest rates in the UK economy are based on the rate set by the bank.

Interest rates in the UK are 5% at the time of writing (October 2008) and are forecast to fall. Other developed economies also have relatively low rates of interest.

Changes in interest rates have significant effects on businesses and the environment in which they operate. They are a central part of monetary policy. For more on this, see pages 99–100.

Reduced consumer spending

Interest rates affect the level of consumer spending in the economy. A rise in interest rates will normally reduce spending by consumers for a number of reasons:

- Consumers are more likely to take a decision to save during a period in which interest rates are rising. The return on their saving is greater and this will persuade some consumers to postpone spending decisions.
- Rising interest rates increase the cost of borrowing. Many goods are purchased on credit, such as electrical goods, cars and caravans, and digital television systems. If rates rise, the cost of purchasing these goods on credit will increase, persuading some people not to buy them.

- Many UK consumers have mortgages. A rise in interest rates will increase the monthly payments of householders and reduce the income available for other expenditure.

A fall in interest rates will tend to increase demand for many products and expenditure will rise. The reverse of the above will take place.

Higher overheads

A rise in interest rates will result in higher overheads for most businesses. For example, a business will encounter greater interest charges on any loans it has taken out. It has been estimated that a 1% rise in interest rates means that small businesses in the UK pay an extra £200 million in interest charges. This could be particularly significant on long-term loans such as mortgages. In times of rising interest rates, firms might limit borrowing (especially short-term borrowing) but may be able to do little about the increased costs of long-term loans.

Postponed investment

Firms may postpone investment decisions at a time of rising interest rates. The cost of borrowing money to finance any project is likely to increase when rates rise, and investments may then become unviable. It may become more attractive to place money with a financial institution, since returns may be significantly greater. Postponement of investment decisions reduces the level of economic activity in the economy. The construction and engineering industries are particularly susceptible to declining order books at such a time.

Higher exchange rate

There is an important link between the domestic rate of interest and the value of a nation's currency. A rise in the UK's rate of interest increases the exchange value of the pound sterling. As interest rates rise in relation to the rates available in other countries, the UK becomes an increasingly attractive target for international investment. Foreigners with money to invest are tempted by the high returns available from UK institutions. However, in order to invest in the UK, foreigners need to purchase pounds. This rise in demand for pounds results in a rise in the exchange rate of the pound. If interest rates fall, the same mechanism operates in reverse (see Table 8.4).

If UK interest rates fall...	If UK interest rates rise...
<ul><li>Foreign investors judge the UK to be a less rewarding place in which to invest their money.</li><li>They decide to withdraw existing investments and/or not to make new ones.</li><li>They sell pounds to purchase the currencies of the countries in which they will now invest their funds.</li><li>The supply of pounds on to the international currency market increases.</li><li>The exchange value of the pound falls against other major currencies.</li></ul>	<ul><li>The UK appears a relatively rewarding location for foreign investors to place their funds.</li><li>Foreign investors decide to invest in UK financial institutions to earn the high rate of interest.</li><li>They sell their own currencies to purchase pounds in order to be able to invest in the UK.</li><li>The demand for pounds increases on the international currency markets.</li><li>The exchange value of the pound rises against other major currencies.</li></ul>

Table 8.4 *The effects of a rise or fall in UK interest rates on the value of the pound*

Exchange rates

An exchange rate is the price of one currency expressed in terms of another. So, on a given day, £1 may be worth US$1.75 or €1.25.

There is a highly developed foreign exchange market in which currencies are bought and sold. London is one of the premier international centres for exchanging foreign currencies, with transactions totalling billions of pounds each day. Exchange rates between most currencies vary regularly according to the balance of supply and demand for each individual currency.

Currencies are exchanged for a number of reasons:
- Firms purchasing products from overseas are expected to pay in the producer's domestic currency. So, a UK firm purchasing Canadian timber will have to change pounds sterling into Canadian dollars to settle its account with the timber exporter, as shown in Figure 8.2.

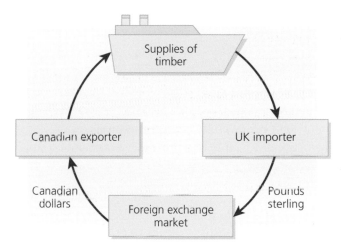

Figure 8.2 How a UK importer buys timber from a Canadian exporter

- Demand for foreign currencies can also arise because individuals and businesses wish to invest in enterprises overseas. Thus, a UK citizen wishing to invest in a Japanese business will require yen to complete the transaction.
- Sometimes governments buy or sell their own currencies if they wish to influence the price or exchange rate. A government decision to use reserves of gold or other foreign currencies to purchase its own currency is likely to increase the exchange rate — provided other people and institutions are not selling huge quantities of the currency. Similarly, selling the currency is likely to depress its exchange value.

Changes in exchange rates have a considerable impact on businesses in the UK. This is true even for those businesses that do not trade overseas. Small changes in the UK's exchange rate occur all the time because it is floating. A series of slight rises and falls over a period of time is not necessarily a major problem for industry. Of more concern is a sustained rise or fall in the exchange rate — or a sudden and substantial change.

Significant changes in the exchange rate can create a number of difficulties for businesses:

- Firms experience difficulty in forecasting earnings from overseas sales in the event of an exchange rate change taking place between agreeing the price (in the foreign currency) and receiving payment. If the pound rises in value, earnings from export sales can decline.
- Costs of imported raw materials can vary because of exchange rate fluctuations. A price quoted to customers might suddenly become unprofitable if the price paid for raw materials from overseas rises.
- Significant exchange rate fluctuations can change the price charged overseas for a product. A rise in the value of the pound makes it more difficult for exporters, while a fall in the value of the pound can help exporters to be more price competitive.

Example

Norris Engineering exports bicycles to the USA. Currently they cost £100 to produce and transport to the USA. With an exchange rate of £1 to $1.50, they can be sold in the USA for $150 plus the retailer's margin. Following a rise in the value of sterling, the exchange rate is £1 = $1.65. The same bicycle will sell in USA for $165 plus the retailer's commission. Sales may fall and Norris Engineering will still receive only £100 for each bicycle sold.

Examiner's tip

When discussing prices (in connection with exchange rates), don't ignore price elasticity. If overseas demand for a product is price inelastic, an increase in the exchange rate may not be too harmful. Rolls-Royce's sales might be relatively unaffected in such circumstances. But the same might not be true of a firm selling engineering components in a highly price-competitive market.

It is important to be able to analyse the effects of a change in the value of the pound on a business. Table 8.5 summarises these changes.

Exchange value of the pound	Prices of UK exports overseas in local currency	Prices of products imported into the UK in pounds sterling
Increases (appreciates)	Rise	Fall
Decreases (depreciates)	Fall	Rise

Table 8.5 The effects on a business of a change in the value of the pound

Changes in exchange rates only affect the price at which imports and exports are sold. A number of other factors influence purchasing decisions in international markets:

- the reputation and quality of the product in question
- the design and functions of the product
- the after-sales service provided
- delivery dates and the business's record in meeting them

Exchange rates are an important issue for businesses selling in price-competitive international markets. In these circumstances, a small change in the exchange rate can eliminate a firm's profit margin or make the firm uncompetitive.

1.2 Trends in key economic variables

You should be aware of the major trends in the following economic variables during your period of studying A2 Business Studies:

- gross national product (GNP)
- inflation as measured by the consumer price index (CPI)
- the level of unemployment (as a percentage of the working population or a total figure)
- the exchange value of the pound against key currencies such as the euro, US dollar and Japanese yen.

It is important that you appreciate the trend in these data — whether it is rising, falling or stable, and how the figures compare with those of other major economies.

The following websites may help you to gain the latest data available:

- **newsvote.bbc.co.uk/1/shared/fds/hi/business/market_data/currency/default.stm**
- **www.bankofengland.co.uk/mfsd/iadb/Index.asp?first=yes&SectionRequired= I&HideNums=-1&ExtraInfo=true&Travel=NIx**
- **www.incomesdata.co.uk/statistics/statempl.htm**

1.3 The globalisation of markets

At its simplest, **globalisation** refers to the trend for many markets to become worldwide in scope. Because of globalisation, many businesses trade throughout the world, whereas in the past they may have focused on one country, or possibly a single continent such as Europe. One of the reasons that globalisation is so controversial is because different groups can interpret it in many different ways.

Fears about globalisation

For some groups, globalisation is a uniquely threatening word. It prompts visions of large multinationals dominating the world, selling Coca-Cola and Big Macs to consumers in pursuit of ever-higher profits. Many pressure groups fear that globalisation threatens the environment as well as national cultures, and predict that it will make the rich nations richer while impoverishing developing countries.

Citizens in rich and poor countries alike see the threat posed to their local cultures by globalisation, and have acted to protect them. For example, Canadian communities are fighting to keep out the giant Wal-Mart chain, for fear that it will destroy neighbourhood shopping centres. Throughout the world, citizens are battling to preserve their cultural identities against the forces of global commerce.

The benefits of globalisation

Of course, many governments and businesses have an entirely different view of globalisation. They believe that increased and freer trade between nations will offer prosperity and growth for all countries and businesses. Globalisation, they argue, has already brought many benefits: global food production has risen steadily over the last 20 years and malnutrition rates have fallen accordingly. Citizens in less developed countries have access to healthcare, often supplied by foreign businesses. For its supporters, globalisation offers an opportunity rather than posing a threat. The leaders of the world's major economies and big businesses are committed to protecting and promoting global commerce and trade, and reject claims of 'cultural imperialism' made against companies such as McDonald's and Coca-Cola.

1.4 Developments in emerging markets

The term **emerging markets** refers to those countries that are experiencing rapid industrialisation and the creation of manufacturing industry that this stage of economic development entails. Examples are China, India, Pakistan, Mexico, Brazil, Chile, Colombia, Argentina, Peru, a number of countries in eastern Europe, and the Middle East.

Economies that are industrialising rapidly are likely to share a number of characteristics:
- rapid increases in the production of manufactured goods
- production of manufactured goods at lower prices
- a steady development (albeit more slowly) of service industries
- an improved infrastructure as transport and communications are extended and developed
- rising incomes for at least some of the population

Opportunities in emerging markets

Emerging markets offer a range of opportunities to businesses in developed countries such as the UK:
- They provide a source of cheap finished products. For example, many of the clothes sold by high-street retailers in the UK are made in China and other Asian countries, where labour costs are much lower.
- Countries such as Brazil have the infrastructure to supply large quantities of raw materials such as copper at relatively low prices, to meet the needs of businesses in the UK and other developed countries.
- Increasingly, emerging markets provide attractive low-cost locations for UK-owned manufacturing businesses. As markets have become global, locating elsewhere in the world has fewer implications in terms of transport costs.

The threat posed by emerging nations

Such nations pose a competitive threat to businesses in the developed world. Low costs of production mean that they are able to be extremely price competitive. Initially, firms in emerging nations only produced relatively low-technology goods, but as time has passed, they have manufactured more sophisticated products and now pose a major threat to established producers. The danger is that some established businesses may be complacent and lose global market share to the 'new' producers.

Demand from businesses in emerging markets has seen rising prices for raw materials such as oil, grain and industrial materials like coal, zinc and copper. This has increased the production costs of most businesses and has led to an upward twist in the rate of inflation.

1.5 The responses of businesses to changes in the economic environment

First, it is important to recognise that changes in the economic environment can offer opportunities as well as posing threats. It is perfectly likely that a change (such as the emergence of China as a major economy) offers both simultaneously. A business may consider a number of responses to economic change:

- **Rationalisation**. This entails reducing the scale of the business, possibly by closing down less profitable elements.
- **Capacity increase or reduction**. A change in the economic environment may increase or reduce demand for a firm's products. Firms may respond by reducing capacity (reducing employees' hours or mothballing factories) or by increasing capacity by subcontracting work to other businesses.
- **Seeking new markets**. Economic change may make other markets more accessible, or more attractive, if the 'home' market suffers from adverse economic change.
- **Producing new products**. Rising incomes may mean that consumers have more money to spend on luxury items. So, for example, travel firms may introduce new long-haul holidays in exotic locations.
- **Mergers and takeovers**. This could be an appropriate response to a variety of economic changes. Larger, more diverse businesses may be better suited to cope with the challenges of globalisation, or the problems of a major international economic downturn.

These are only a few possible responses to economic change. The exact responses will depend on the precise circumstances of the business and may vary enormously between businesses. For example, the onset of recession in the UK in 2008 led to the closure of Woolworths while another retailer, Morrisons, announced healthy profits and considered buying some of Woolworths' premises.

2 *The relationship between businesses and the political and legal environment*

What you need to know:
- how the government intervenes in the economy
- the nature and range of government economic policies
- political decisions affecting trade and access to markets
- the impact of legislation relating to businesses
- the responses of businesses to changes in the political and legal environment

This topic also requires you to evaluate the strategies that businesses might deploy in response to these changes. We will consider a range of strategies as we look at the various political and legal factors that can cause change at the end of this section.

2.1 How the government intervenes in the economy

Government provision of products
UK central and local government provides a range of products, including:
- healthcare
- education
- defence
- policing
- library services
- refuse disposal

In some cases the government supplies these services because it is impractical for private organisations to do so, as in the case of defence. In other circumstances, they are provided free of charge to the user to prevent the products being under-consumed. Health and education are examples of such products.

Regulation of markets

Regulation means that the government intervenes in the operation of the market. For example, the government created Ofgem to promote competition and to control the monopoly companies that run the gas and electricity networks. Ofgem encourages gas and electricity suppliers to take environmentally friendly decisions and to look after the interests of vulnerable customers such as the disabled and elderly. Organisations such as Ofgem can have a considerable impact on markets if consumers are aware of them and their roles, and if sufficient budgets are available to allow them to conduct their roles effectively.

Taxation and subsidy

In other cases, the government intervenes in the supply of products through taxation. Tobacco and alcohol are taxed in part to discourage consumption of these harmful products and in part to raise revenue for the government. In contrast, the government offers subsidies to encourage the production of green energy, such as electricity generated by wind farms.

The extent to which taxation and subsidies may affect consumers' and producers' decisions will depend to some extent on the price elasticity of demand for the product.

2.2 The nature and range of government economic policies

The government implements a series of policies designed to provide a stable and prosperous economic environment for businesses. Successive governments have argued that an appropriate economic environment would show the following characteristics:

- steady and sustained economic growth, avoiding the worst booms and slumps associated with the trade cycle
- price stability
- low rates of unemployment
- a stable exchange rate for the pound

Fiscal policy

Fiscal policy refers to government policies based on taxation and its own expenditure.

Taxation

The UK has two broad categories of taxes:

- direct taxes, levied on income and capital (e.g. income tax)
- indirect taxes, levied on expenditure (e.g. value added tax)

The government can raise the level of economic activity in the UK by lowering the rates of taxation. The chancellor of the exchequer usually announces changes in the rates of taxation during the Budget speech. The effects of such changes are outlined in Table 8.6.

It is relatively easy to forecast the impact of changes in taxation rates on the overall level of economic activity. But the effects of these changes vary between individual firms. Businesses producing price-elastic goods will be affected by changes in indirect taxes, as demand is sensitive to price. Those firms producing income-elastic products may find their sales more affected by alterations in the rates of direct taxation. Firms supplying products such as foreign holidays or jewellery will be sensitive to changes in consumers' incomes; those selling basic foodstuffs are less likely to be affected.

The effects of increases in taxation	The effects of reductions in taxation
• Increases in indirect taxes such as VAT result in higher prices, cutting consumer demand. • Producers may pay the increase in indirect taxes to avoid raising prices; this will cut profits and may reduce investment levels by businesses. • Increases in income tax leave consumers with less disposable income, again reducing demand.	• Cutting indirect taxes reduces prices, which may boost spending — especially for price-elastic products. • Reductions in income tax result in consumers having higher levels of disposable income. This increases demand, particularly for income-elastic products. • Falling corporate taxation promotes investment and output by businesses, increasing economic activity. • Reductions in corporate taxation may attract inward investment by foreign individuals and businesses, promoting prosperity.

Table 8.6 The effects of increases and reductions in taxation

Government expenditure

Government expenditure is the other part of fiscal policy. It can be placed in two categories:

• **Transfer payments.** This is government spending on pensions, unemployment benefit and similar social security payments. Alterations in this category of government expenditure have a rapid and significant impact on consumers' spending and the level of economic activity. Recipients are generally not well off and need to spend the money to maintain their standard of living.

• **Spending on the nation's infrastructure.** This is spending on such things as roads, schools, bridges and harbours. This type of expenditure can have a double impact on businesses. First, the results of the expenditure can enhance the environment for firms by improving communications and cutting the costs of transportation. Second, the construction can provide work and income for firms, so boosting their profitability. The government can also encourage investment by companies through offering investment grants and tax relief (see Table 8.7).

	Falling level of economic activity	Rising level of economic activity
Caused by	Reduced government spending or increased taxation.	Increased government expenditure or lower rates of taxation.
Likely effects	Increased unemployment, declining spending and production.	Inflation may appear while unemployment falls as imports increase.
Impact on business	Falling sales and downward pressure on prices. Rising numbers of bankruptcies, especially among small firms. Increased levels of inventories.	Rising wages and possible skill shortages. Sales rise and possibility of increasing prices. Increasing costs of raw materials and components.

Table 8.7 Fiscal policy and levels of economic activity

Monetary policy

Monetary policy centres on adjusting the amount of money in circulation and hence the level of spending and economic activity. Monetary policy can make use of one or more of the following:

- altering interest rates
- controlling the money supply
- manipulating the exchange rate

Although at times all three techniques have been used, recent governments have tended to adopt neutral fiscal policies and to rely on adjusting interest rates to manage the economy. We saw earlier that interest rate policy has been controlled by the Monetary Policy Committee of the Bank of England since 1997.

Broadly speaking, rises in interest rates depress the level of economic activity and reductions promote an expansion of economic activity. A rise in the level of interest rates in the UK will reduce the level of economic activity for a number of reasons:

- Individuals and businesses will tend to save more, so reducing the level of expenditure and production.
- Consumers will postpone or abandon plans to purchase goods on credit, as interest charges have risen.
- Businesses will take decisions to reduce investment plans, as the cost of borrowing has risen and fewer projects will be viable.
- Firms may reduce inventory levels in an attempt to reduce their need to borrow to obtain working capital.
- Trade credit will become more expensive and firms will seek to offer less credit (at the same time as they attempt to gain more).
- There may be upward pressure on costs, as firms face higher charges to service their long-term debt. This may result in increases in retail prices.
- Firms may encounter (and have to make provision for) higher levels of bad debts.
- There will be an increase in the exchange value of the pound through the mechanism outlined earlier. This will increase the price of UK exports while reducing the price of imports.

The impact of rising interest rates will depend on the size of the change as well as the initial rate. A small increase at a relatively high level of rates will have little impact, while a larger increase from a low base rate will have a significant impact. As the economies of the European Union become more integrated, EU interest rates will become more influential on the behaviour of businesses.

Supply-side policies

Policies designed to promote greater and more efficient markets and production have gained credence over recent years. They attempt to improve the working of the economy by improving the operation of free markets. The main elements of supply-side policies are:

- **Improving the quality of the labour force.** This can be done through increasing training to provide a more committed and skilled labour force. The Investors in People (IIP) scheme is an integral part of this approach.
- **Limiting the power of trade unions.** One reason for restricting the power of trade unions has been to make the labour market work more effectively and to avoid the excessive wage increases and limited increases in productivity that some people associate with the exercise of trade union power.
- **Reducing labour costs.** By making the labour market work effectively, the government hopes to allow wages to reflect local conditions. However, the introduction of the minimum wage since 1999 has imposed an artificial constraint on the operation of labour markets.

2.3 Political decisions affecting trade and access to markets

Political decisions by governments can have significant impacts on businesses and their trading activities.

- **Freeing entry to markets.** Decisions such as the one by the UK government to allow other businesses to compete with Royal Mail in the delivery of letters have had significant implications for the business community and for consumers. This has permitted the entry of new businesses such as Business Post and has offered consumers (and especially other businesses) choice.

- **Encouraging international trade.** Governments can work together to take decisions such as reducing or removing tariffs (taxes on imports), and thereby encouraging trade between different countries. The World Trade Organization exists to promote international trade. Similarly, the creation of economic groupings of countries such as the European Union will assist in promoting trade and allow the creation of what are effectively larger markets. This offers a range of benefits to businesses, including economies of scale.

- **Decisions to improve infrastructure.** A country's infrastructure is its road and rail networks and other communication systems. Governments often take decisions to invest in improving these aspects of a country's stock of capital. In general, these offer positive short- and long-term benefits to businesses. Some businesses benefit from undertaking profitable work to improve the infrastructure at the government's request. In the longer term, other businesses benefit from being able to use the infrastructure and to trade more efficiently as a consequence.

2.4 The impact of legislation relating to businesses

The European Union and the UK government play a major role in determining the environment in which firms operate, by implementing a range of legislation that affects businesses. The EU has an increasing role in passing laws (known as **directives**) that influence the activities of UK businesses. In the case of any conflict between EU and UK law, the legislation of the European Union takes precedence.

The key areas of legislation that affect business are:
- health and safety
- employment protection
- consumer protection
- environmental protection
- competition policy

Examiner's tip

It is important in this area of the specification to concentrate on the impact of legislation on businesses and their possible responses to changes in the legal environment. Don't spend long periods learning the content of the various laws. A broad appreciation of the nature and scope of the relevant legislation is all that is required.

Health and safety legislation

Health and safety legislation has been enacted to discourage dangerous practices by businesses and to protect the workforce. The legislation focuses on the prevention of accidents. The main act in the UK is the Health and Safety at Work Act (1974). This is an example of **delegated legislation**, whereby parliament delegates responsibility to government departments to produce 'statutory instruments' to update the scope of the legislation as necessary. This ensures that legislation is relevant while not taking up too much of parliament's time.

The main provisions of the Health and Safety at Work Act are designed to 'ensure as far as is reasonably practical' the health and safety of all staff at work. The provisions of the Act include the following:

- All employees are obliged to follow safety rules and regulations.
- Firms must display a written safety policy.
- Businesses should provide necessary safety equipment free of charge.
- Safety representatives have the right to investigate workplace accidents and conduct the inspections necessary to ensure a safe workplace.

The UK's health and safety legislation is continuously updated under the provisions of the Health and Safety at Work Act to take account of changes in working practices. For example, in December 2002 health and safety legislation relating to explosive substances in the workplace was strengthened following a number of accidents.

In addition, the European Union has enacted health and safety legislation relating to pregnant workers, the length of the working week and the use of computers in the workplace.

Health and safety legislation is an important issue for firms operating in the primary and secondary sectors of the economy. For example, construction companies impose rigorous health and safety policies and monitor incidents very closely to avoid their repetition.

Examiner's tip

You should be aware of the key terms in this area of the specification. Terms worthy of research include: **cartels**, **restrictive practices**, **voluntary codes of practice** and **oligopolies**. Understanding important terms allows you to answer definition questions with confidence, but also to use these words as a form of shorthand when developing analytical and evaluative answers.

Employment protection

Employment protection falls into two categories: individual labour law and collective labour law.

Individual labour law

This category of legislation grants protection to, and places obligations on, individuals. Some key pieces of legislation are as follows:

- Discrimination on grounds of sex in employment and education is unlawful under the **Sex Discrimination Acts (1975, 1986)** as reinforced by the **Employment Act (1989)**.
- The **Equal Pay Act (1970)** states that sexes should be treated equally. A woman employed in the same job as a man must have the same pay and conditions of employment.

- The **Race Relations Act (1976)** makes it unlawful to discriminate in relation to employment on the grounds of sex, marital status, colour or race.
- The **Disability Discrimination Act (1995)** makes it illegal for an employer to treat a disabled person less favourably than others.
- The **National Minimum Wage Act (1998)** is a highly publicised Act that came into force on 1 April 1999. The key features of the new legislation are a general minimum wage of £4.20 per hour and a minimum level of £3.60 an hour for 18–21-year-olds (2002 rates). All part-time and temporary workers must be paid the minimum wage.
- The **Working Time Regulations (1998)** are EU legislation, limiting the hours that employees can be required to work each week to 48 hours. Employees can choose to work longer hours, but employers cannot insist that they do so without inserting an appropriate clause in their contract of employment.

Collective labour law

This legislation relates to industrial relations and trade union activities. Some relevant pieces of recent legislation are outlined below.

The **Employment Protection (Consolidation) Act (1978)** covers a number of aspects:
- **Contracts of employment.** All employees working more than 16 hours per week must be given a contract of employment by their employer within 13 weeks of starting work.
- **Dismissal of employees.** Once employed for 4 weeks, employees are entitled to a minimum of 1 week's notice. After 2 years, this increases to a period of 1 week for each year's service up to a maximum of 12 weeks.
- **Dismissal procedures.** Normally an employee is given a verbal warning of unsatisfactory conduct or performance, followed by a written warning if appropriate. If the problem remains, there may be a formal hearing at which the employee may be represented by his or her trade union.

A whole series of industrial relations legislation has been passed, starting with the **Industrial Relations Act (1971)**, to influence negotiations between employers and employees. These have included the following Acts:
- **Employment Act (1980).** This enabled firms to derecognise unions. It also restricted picketing to employees' 'own place of work'.
- **Trade Union Act (1984).** This made a secret ballot of employees mandatory before industrial action was lawful.
- **Employment Act (1988).** This protected union members from being disciplined by unions for ignoring strike calls.
- **Employment Act (1990).** This reduced the likelihood of unofficial strikes by permitting employers to dismiss workers taking this form of action. The Act effectively ended closed-shop agreements. It made it illegal to refuse to employ an individual because he or she is not a member of a union.
- **Trade Union Reform and Employment Rights Act (1993).** This required unions to provide employers with at least 7 days' notice of official industrial action. It also abolished wages councils and their imposition of minimum pay rates.
- **Employment Relations Act (1999).** This established legal guidelines for union recognition by employers in businesses with over 21 employees as well as granting up to 3 months' parental leave to mothers and fathers. Finally, in a minor reversal of some earlier legislation, it extended the legal protection given to workers taking industrial action.

Consumer protection

Consumer protection encompasses a series of Acts designed to safeguard consumers against unfair trading practices and dangerous products. This is managed by the Office of Fair Trading, which also looks after competition policy. The legislation already in place is outlined below.

- **Sale of Goods Act (1979).** The basic requirement is that the seller must ensure that the goods sold are satisfactory. They must be of merchantable quality — that is, they must be undamaged and unbroken, and must work properly; they must also be fit for the particular purpose and as described by the manufacturer.
- **Consumer Protection Act (1987).** This states that producers can be held liable for harm caused by their products.

Other important Acts include the following:

- **Food Safety Act (1990)** — to ensure the safety of food.
- **Trade Descriptions Act (1968)** — misleading descriptions of goods/services are an offence.
- **Weights and Measures (1963 and 1985)** — weights and measures given must be accurate.
- **Consumer Credit Act (1974)** — credit can be given only by licensed organisations.

Increases in the scope of consumer protection have had a number of implications for businesses:

- **The costs of production have risen.** Meeting the requirements of, for example, weights and measures and consumer credit entails additional processes and personnel, thereby increasing costs.
- **There is greater emphasis on supplying products of consistently high quality.** Firms are vulnerable to prosecution for supplying substandard items and wish to avoid any adverse publicity in this respect.
- **Consumerism is now a force to be reckoned with.** Consumers have become more knowledgeable and discerning in their purchases. They often conduct research (aided by publications such as *Which?*) before making major purchases.

Environmental protection

The government has passed a series of Acts of Parliament designed to protect the environment. Two are particularly important:

- **Environmental Protection Act (1991).** This introduced the notion of integrated pollution control, recognising that to control only a single source of pollution is worthless, as damage to one part of the environment means damage to it all. This Act requires business to minimise pollution as a whole.
- **Environment Act (1995).** This legislation established the Environment Agency with the brief of coordinating and overseeing environmental protection. The Act also covered the control of pollution and the conservation of the environment, and made provision for restoring contaminated land and abandoned mines.

The government imposes fines on firms that breach legislation relating to the protection of the environment. These are intended to force firms to bear the full costs of their production (including external costs), although environmental pressure groups and other critics believe that the sums are not sufficient to deter major businesses with budgets of billions of pounds annually.

The government also attempts to encourage 'greener' methods of production through the provision of grants. The government has created the Carbon Trust, which since April 2001 has given capital grants to firms that invest in energy-saving technologies. The intention is to slow the onset of global warming by reducing emissions of carbon dioxide. In a similar vein, government funding is also supporting the development of environmentally friendly offshore wind farms to generate 'clean' electricity.

Competition policy

Competition policy deals with monopolies, mergers and restrictive practices. A **monopoly** can be defined as 'a situation where there are no close substitutes for the goods that a firm produces'. The result of monopolies could be that:

- consumers are exploited through excessive prices
- consumers are offered a poor service
- some firms face unfair competition

A number of safeguards against such exploitation exist. These include:

- **Greater competition.** For example, since privatisation British Telecom (BT) has not had a monopoly in supplying telephone equipment.
- **The formation of 'watchdog' organisations.** These include Oftel, which monitors complaints from telecommunications customers.
- **The Office of Fair Trading and the Competition Commission.** These bodies ensure that firms with a large share of the market do not act against the public interest; proposed mergers are investigated, competition is encouraged and restrictive practices are discouraged. The Competition Commission was previously called the Monopolies and Mergers Commission.
- **The Restrictive Practices Court.** This considers cases involving **restrictive practices** — that is, business practices that reduce the degree of competition. These include creating **cartels** that set high prices or other adverse conditions of sale.
- **The Data Protection Act (1984).** This is designed to prevent businesses abusing the power and access to information which computers and databases give them. It is most applicable to information processed by computer. Such data cannot be used or disclosed in any manner incompatible with the purpose for which the information is held.

2.5 The responses of businesses to changes in the political and legal environment

This book can only give you a few prompts to consider in regard to how businesses respond to changes in the political and legal environment. The precise responses of a business will depend on a number of factors, including the type and size of the business, its objectives, the nature and competitiveness of the market in which it trades and the extent to which the proposed or actual change will affect it.

Political and legal changes can offer opportunities as well as imposing constraints on the activities of businesses. Legislation relating to minimum wage or discrimination is likely to constrain the activities of firms. However, in contrast, new markets have been created for businesses supplying training in environmental management. Firms also offer to supply environmental control equipment to minimise the possibility of environmental harm during production. Equally, a market exists for testing equipment to monitor emissions or the toxicity of waste products. Finally, businesses can use environmental policies as a means of obtaining a competitive advantage. BMW, for example,

promotes itself as a manufacturer of cars that are almost entirely recyclable. This could prove attractive to environmentally aware consumers.

Examiner's tip

In an examination, think about the precise nature of the business about which you are writing in detail. You might like to ask questions such as:
- What are the financial implications of this change? Does the business have sufficient finance available to respond effectively?
- Does the change affect the particular market or markets in which the business trades?
- Will the change offer a marketing opportunity?
- Does the change help or hinder the business in achieving its corporate objectives?
- Does the change have a greater impact on the business than on its major competitors?

3 The relationship between businesses and the social environment

What you need to know:
- the nature of changes in the social environment
- the changing nature of the ethical environment
- the responses of businesses to changes in the social environment, including corporate social responsibility

3.1 The nature of changes in the social environment

Social factors have a considerable impact on the behaviour of businesses. Over recent years, many changes in social attitudes have been highlighted by the activities of pressure groups. Important issues have included:
- the desire among consumers to purchase environmentally friendly products
- increasing concern expressed about the treatment of farm animals and a greater number of consumers opting to become vegetarians
- a demand for firms to meet the needs of other stakeholder groups apart from shareholders
- the increasing number of single-person households and their different patterns of demand

A business's social responsibilities are the duties it has towards its stakeholders — employees, customers and society at large — as well as towards its shareholders (see Figure 8.3). Some firms willingly embrace these responsibilities, while others reject them.

Those who support the **stakeholder concept** recognise that a business has to aim to satisfy the needs of all groups that have an interest in the organisation. The **shareholder concept** argues that businesses exist to meet the needs of shareholders for profits and that decisions should reflect this objective.

A business may accept its social responsibilities for two reasons:
- It has a genuine belief in the stakeholder concept, which recognises the needs of all parties with an interest in the organisation.
- It believes that it can derive some positive publicity from being seen to be socially responsible.

Figure 8.3 The stakeholders of a business

Increasingly, firms are being asked to consider and justify their actions towards a wide range of groups rather than just their shareholders. A number of issues arise as a result of these pressures:

- Even firms that have a genuine desire to change may experience difficulties in altering their existing culture. It may take years to establish a genuine stakeholder culture.
- The stakeholder approach can lead to many benefits for organisations. These include: keeping existing customers and winning new ones; recruiting and keeping high-quality employees; and developing a positive long-term corporate image.
- The precise social responsibilities that a firm should meet vary from business to business and change over time. However, consumers increasingly expect businesses to meet their social responsibilities.

It is unlikely that a business will be able to meet the needs of all interest groups. It is normal for some sort of trade-off to take place. By fulfilling the needs of one stakeholder group, the demands of others may be ignored. In a time of slump, when profits are reduced, businesses may be more likely to focus on meeting the needs of shareholders. In more prosperous periods, a broader range of stakeholders may be satisfied.

Social responsibilities are particularly important for some types of business. For example, firms producing relatively undifferentiated products may opt to meet social responsibilities as fully as possible in order to provide a unique selling proposition.

Demographic changes

The population in the UK is changing in a number of ways:

- **Population growth.** The population of the UK is growing. In 2007 it passed 60 million and it is forecast to grow steadily, as shown in Figure 8.4 overleaf. This offers sales opportunities to businesses and also a greater supply of labour. Indeed, one of the driving forces behind the population growth has been the inflow of migrants from eastern Europe. This has helped to keep the growth of wages at a low level.
- **An ageing population.** The UK, along with most of Western Europe, is experiencing an increase in the average age of its population. In 2000 there were 11.2 million people under the age of 15 in the UK; by 2040, this will have fallen to 8.7 million. Over the same period, the number of people over 64 in is expected to grow from 9.5 million to 15 million. In 1999 the working population amounted to 47.8% of the total UK population. By 2030 it will be 44.5%. These changes will have significant

implications for the supply of labour available to businesses as well as the pattern of products that consumers demand.

- **An increasing number of households.** The number of households (that is, separate homes) in the UK has increased steadily over recent years, fuelling an increased demand not only for property, but also for consumer durables such as furniture and electrical products. One eye-catching statistic is that the number of single-person households has risen by more than 25% since 1991. This has led to food manufacturers, for example, supplying their products in smaller quantities.
- **The cultural make-up of the UK.** The UK has become a far more multicultural country over the last 50 years as a result of migration, initially from the Indian subcontinent and more recently from eastern Europe and parts of Africa. This has prompted a changing pattern of demand for goods and services. A prime example has been the change in restaurants that has accompanied the inflow of migrants.

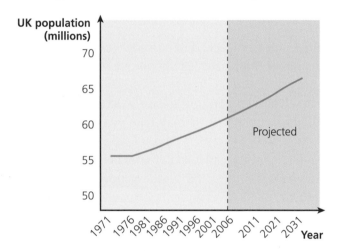

Figure 8.4 UK population growth

Source: BBC News (http://news.bbc.co.uk/1/hi/uk/5281360.stm)

Environmental issues

Businesses face a number of issues in relation to the environment:

- global warming, whereby excessive production and release of CFCs and carbon dioxide is damaging the protective layer of ozone that exists in the upper atmosphere
- pollution of the atmosphere, resulting in smog and acid rain, which are harmful to both individuals and the environment
- the need to recycle products such as paper and metal to avoid the problem of disposing of vast quantities of waste as well as using up precious natural resources
- using sustainable sources for products such as timber to avoid unnecessary depletion of the world's natural resources

Environmental standards exist in much the same way as quality standards across the globe. The environmental standards are regulated by the International Standards Organization and exist to highlight and confirm good practice by businesses. Table 8.8 outlines the potential benefits and costs for businesses in meeting environmental standards.

Environmental issues are important for manufacturing businesses and particularly those with considerable potential to pollute the atmosphere. This is particularly true if the business sells directly to the public. Companies such as Shell and BP Amoco fall into this category and have to be especially careful about their public image with regard to environmental issues.

Potential benefits	Potential costs
• Firms may find it easier to raise funds if they have a good environmental record. For example, the Co-operative bank will not lend money to businesses that damage the environment.	• Meeting strict environmental controls imposes additional costs on businesses, as they need to introduce new processes, retrain employees and use more expensive resources.
• Working for a business that genuinely cares about the environment can motivate employees and make it easier to recruit high-calibre staff.	• For a business to be sincere in protecting the environment, it is important for all employees to pursue this objective — it is not always easy to change the culture of a business.
• There are significant marketing advantages to be gained from adopting an environmentally friendly stance. The publicity given to environmental audits by many companies reflects this factor.	• Proper disposal of harmful by-products from manufacturing can be very expensive and may reduce profits to the dismay of shareholders.

Table 8.8 The environmental balance sheet

3.2 The changing nature of the ethical environment

What are ethics?

Ethics can be defined as a code of behaviour considered morally correct. Business ethics can provide moral guidelines for decision making by organisations. Taking an ethical decision means doing what is morally right. It is not simply taking the decision that leads to the highest profits. Many activities in the business world have an ethical dimension. Here are some examples:

- Should a manufacturing business use a cheap, non-sustainable source of timber or a more expensive, sustainable supply that would mean lower profits for shareholders?
- Should a retail chain recruit and train employees or simply poach them from a rival business by offering slightly higher wages?
- If a business is faced by declining demand, should it make its workers redundant immediately or consider retraining them or seeing whether demand picks up in the near future?
- Should a distributor accept a profitable contract to transport tobacco products, in the knowledge that they are damaging to the health of the public?

The actions underpinning these questions are not illegal, but many people would regard them as morally wrong (see Figure 8.5). Whether a business would turn down profitable (or cost-saving) opportunities such as these is debatable.

The law protects society from the worst excesses of business behaviour. Thus, competition legislation prevents monopolies abusing their power, and employment protection legislation looks after the welfare of workers. Ethical behaviour requires businesses to take this process a step further.

Ethical or morally acceptable behaviour requires businesses to reject potentially profitable activities because they have an unacceptable dimension. A food manufacturer, for example, might decide not to use supplies of genetically modified flour in bread, even though traditional sources are significantly more expensive. It would not be illegal to use the genetically modified materials, but the directors of the business may not consider this a morally correct course of action. Ethical behaviour offers benefits to business as well as imposing additional costs, as shown in Table 8.9.

Figure 8.5 *The law and ethical behaviour by businesses*

Advantages	Disadvantages
• There are obvious benefits to a business that is perceived by the public as ethically correct. This may result in increased sales. • Having a positive ethical stance may assist a business in recruiting high-quality employees. It may also result in a lower turnover of staff.	• Taking ethical decisions can be expensive. It may involve turning down highly profitable trading opportunities in favour of taking moral decisions. • There may be conflict with existing staff or existing policies. For example, a policy of delegation may pose problems when attempting to promote a more ethical culture.

Table 8.9 *Advantages and disadvantages of ethical behaviour*

Why can it be difficult for businesses to behave ethically?

Ethically correct behaviour is not always easy to implement throughout an organisation for the following reasons:

- Senior managers may decide to adopt an ethical stance, but persuading other employees to follow their lead can be difficult. Furthermore, shareholders might be dissatisfied if dividends fall as a result of the company taking ethical decisions.
- Firms that practise empowerment and delegation can experience problems in creating an ethical culture, as decision making is in the hands of a large number of employees. A potential conflict exists between ethical behaviour and delegation if budgets are delegated. In these circumstances, junior employees may be reluctant to take less profitable courses of action.
- What one person considers morally correct may be abhorred by others. The development and implementation of a culture acceptable to all can be problematic.

Actions to promote ethical behaviour

Businesses can take the following actions to promote ethical behaviour:

- **Training.** Businesses cannot expect employees automatically to operate within strict moral guidelines. It is important to communicate these guidelines and to prepare employees for decisions that are regarded as morally correct.
- **Consistency.** Businesses need to develop an ethical code of practice to which employees will be expected to adhere. Some businesses (e.g. Texas Instruments) issue documents to encourage ethical behaviour by all employees.

Why has the ethical environment changed?

A number of external influences and organisations encourage businesses to adopt high ethical standards:

- The **Cadbury Committee Report (1992)** called for greater morality in corporate decision making. One of the recommendations of the committee was to reinforce the role of non-executive directors, in the hope that they would ensure greater morality at senior levels in businesses.
- The **Institute of Business Ethics** was established to promote moral behaviour by businesses across the globe. The institute advises businesses on the actions necessary to operate within a positive moral framework, including how to develop an ethical code of practice.
- **Commercial pressures** have encouraged the adoption of ethical cultures by many businesses, especially in sectors such as the oil industry that have significant potential to pollute. Some businesses, notably the Co-operative Bank, have adopted an ethical stance to provide a unique selling proposition in a market with little differentiation between products.

Examiner's tip

There is obvious potential for setting evaluative questions in this area. There are clear commercial advantages resulting from adopting an ethical stance, principally in the field of marketing. At the same time, a business is likely to incur additional costs and possible internal conflict. The net benefit may therefore depend upon factors such as:
- the skill with which the policy is implemented
- the timescale over which the policy is assessed — benefits may take time to become apparent
- the possible reactions of competitors to the policy

Is ethical behaviour genuine?

Some businesses adopt an ethical stance for genuine reasons. Companies such as The Body Shop and the Co-operative Bank have based much of their marketing on their strong moral principles. The beliefs of senior managers may have shaped this policy and helped to give conviction to the stance. While the move may have proved profitable, as in the case of the Co-operative Bank, it is possible in these cases to argue that morals have nevertheless been put before profits.

Other companies may have adopted an apparently ethical stance to improve the public's perception of the business and, ultimately, its profits. To adopt an ethical stance for public relations reasons is a dangerous policy. It may result in the policy being exposed by the media as a sham, with consequent damage to the business's corporate image.

3.3 Responses of businesses to changes in the social environment, including corporate social responsibility

Corporate social responsibility (CSR) is a concept whereby organisations consider the interests of society by taking responsibility for the impact of their activities on customers, suppliers, employees, shareholders, communities and other stakeholders, as well as the environment. This obligation is seen to extend beyond the statutory obligation to comply with legislation, and sees businesses voluntarily taking further steps to improve the quality of life for employees and their families as well as for the local community and society at large.

CSR has been much criticised. Supporters put the business case for CSR, arguing that businesses benefit in multiple ways by operating with a perspective beyond short-term profits. Critics argue that CSR distracts from the fundamental economic role of businesses to make profits and keep shareholders content. Some people believe that CSR is only superficial window-dressing

As part of CSR, businesses use social and environmental audits to set objectives, to measure and to publicise the extent to which they operate in the interests of society at large.

Social audits

A **social audit** is an independent investigation into a firm's activities and its impact on society. Social audits cover pollution, waste and recycling materials. A social audit may be for internal consumption to assist managers in implementing socially responsible policies. Alternatively, or additionally, it may be used externally to project the image of a caring and responsible organisation, in the hope of attracting additional sales.

Social audits provide some indication of the efficiency of a business that cannot be expressed in financial terms. They may provide information on:
- the amount of recycling undertaken by the business
- measures of pollution generated by manufacturing processes
- industrial accidents occurring
- security of employment offered to the local community

Environmental audits

Many businesses, including Shell, BP and The Body Shop, are conducting environmental audits to measure the impact of their operations on the environment. These are similar in nature to social audits but focus specifically on issues such as pollution and waste disposal. These audits can provide useful data for managers in their decision making, as well as contributing positively to a business's corporate image.

Environmental pressures impose costs on businesses but also offer the following opportunities:
- Firms identify niche markets, developing products such as organic vegetables.
- Some businesses utilise the (allegedly) environmentally friendly nature of their processes and products as a unique selling point.
- Selling environmentally friendly products frequently offers businesses the opportunity to charge a premium price.
- By being seen to operate in a manner designed to safeguard the environment, businesses can gain a positive image and enhance sales.

4 The relationship between businesses and the technological environment

What you need to know:
- the effects of technological change
- the responses of businesses to changes in the technological environment

4 *The relationship between businesses and the technological environment*

4.1 The effects of technological change

Technology is advancing at an ever-increasing rate and affects both processes and products. Technological developments include:

- more advanced and sophisticated computers
- the use of nanotechnology in a range of products
- third-generation (3G) mobile telephones
- computer-aided design (CAD) and computer-aided manufacture (CAM)

As the list above shows, technological advances have created new products, new ways of producing products and new ways of selling products. For example, changes in technology mean that more powerful and technologically sophisticated computers are manufactured regularly. But advances in technology mean that computers can be sold in different ways. One of the world's leading manufacturers, Dell, sells its products via the internet rather than through high street retailers. This keeps costs to a minimum, boosting profitability.

Developments in technology have dramatically improved the process of production for many firms — services as well as manufacturing. The development of computer-aided design has made new products easier to design, store and alter. Modern software can also be used to estimate the cost of newly designed products. Technology has revolutionised manufacturing too. Computer-aided manufacturing is used by manufacturing firms of all sizes. Computers control the machines on the production line, saving labour and costs, and CAM systems can be linked to CAD technology to transform the entire process.

Benefits of new technology

New technology offers businesses and consumers a range of benefits:

- Reduced unit costs of production, enhancing the competitiveness of the business concerned. For example, Boeing, the US aircraft manufacturer, designs much of its new aircraft on computers and can assemble 'virtual aircraft'. This reduces the company's use of expensive prototypes.
- In the case of high-technology products, such as new games consoles, the opportunity to charge a premium price until the competition catches up. Such price skimming is likely to boost profits.
- New markets: for example, the internet allows online bookshops to sell worldwide.

Costs of new technology

New technology also poses difficulties for many businesses. For example:

- It is likely to be a drain on an organisation's capital. In some circumstances (e.g. when experiencing high gearing), firms may experience difficulty in raising the funds necessary to install high-technology equipment or to research a new product.
- It inevitably requires training of the existing workforce and perhaps recruitment of new employees. Both actions can create considerable costs for businesses.
- Its introduction may be met with opposition from existing employees, especially if job security is threatened. This may lead to industrial action.

4.2 The responses of businesses to changes in the technological environment

Developing new products

Some businesses have based their corporate strategies on the development of new technology. Apple is well known for its innovative products, even though it does not commit huge sums of money to research and development. Other businesses, such as

Microsoft, deploy the same corporate strategy, embracing technological change and using it as the key element in selling their products. In this way, these companies use technological change to enhance their products. Apple's iPod is a good example of one of the most successful manipulations of a change in technology to the benefit of a business.

Adopting new processes

Technology offers businesses the opportunity to improve the efficiency of their operations process. Thus rapid advances in communications technology have allowed UK banks to set up call centres in India where wage costs are much lower than in the UK. This move has reduced the cost of providing bank accounts or other financial products, thereby reducing the costs of production of the businesses concerned.

Technology has also been used extensively by manufacturers to improve the performance of their businesses. Boeing, one of the world's largest aircraft manufacturers, designs its new aircraft virtually (i.e. on computers), making sure the various parts will fit and operate together. Changes and alterations can be made before any element of the product is actually manufactured. This reduces both costs and the likelihood of expensive errors once production commences.

Using traditional approaches to develop a USP

Some businesses deliberately avoid the technological approach to production or to the resulting products. For example, the traditional wooden toy market has survived despite fierce competition from products incorporating the latest technology. Some banks advertise that they have a bank manager whom you can meet and speak with. Their stance is that you will not always be dealing with technology. Banks using this approach hope to gain a competitive advantage.

5 | *The relationship between businesses and the competitive environment*

What you need to know:
- the effects of changes in the competitive structure of markets
- the responses of businesses to changes in the competitive environment

5.1 The effects of changes in the competitive structure of markets

The arrival of new competitors

New competitors can have a number of effects on a market:
- **Driving prices down.** This has been the situation in the European air travel market since the arrival of easyJet and Ryanair. It can encourage existing businesses to offer more competitive prices or to develop strategies to differentiate themselves from the new businesses. This may benefit consumers but could also lead to diminished quality if profit margins are slim.
- **New products offering customers additional choices and possibly extending the market.** The G-Wiz electric car has been designed for city driving and to be environmentally friendly. The car was designed in California and is manufactured by the Indo-US Reva Electric Car Company. It may have resulted in fewer sales for existing car manufacturers, but may also have developed a new niche market in which existing producers may compete. So, a new competitor can stimulate a market.

- **The closure of some existing producers.** The least efficient producers in the market may not survive the entry of new, more competitive businesses. This can reduce consumer choice and may result in a few large businesses dominating a market.

The creation of dominant businesses

There is a trend in many markets, especially global markets, towards fewer, larger businesses. Many such markets are becoming oligopolistic in nature. Alex Trotman, the former chief executive of Ford, the US car manufacturer, forecast that the global car market in the twenty-first century would eventually have three large car manufacturers: one in Europe, one in North America and one in Asia. Current changes in the market suggest that his prophecy might become reality.

Firms can become dominant in markets through **mergers** (joining with other businesses) or through **takeovers** when one business purchases control of another. The resulting business will be larger and will have greater influence in the market. It will be more able to influence market prices, to exercise control over supplies of materials and components, or to invest in research and development to create new products and processes.

Changes in the buying power of customers

As some businesses increase in scale, they can become the largest or even sole customers of other businesses. It is not uncommon for supermarkets in the UK to be the sole customers of farmers or other food producers. This gives the supermarkets a powerful hand in negotiating prices and contract terms. Dairy farmers, in particular, have argued that they have been forced to supply milk at prices below the cost of production. This change might benefit the final consumer in the short term if low prices are passed on, but if the suppliers go out of business, this could create long-term shortages in the supply industry.

Possessing considerable buying power can be a major advantage to a business if it is selling its products in a price-competitive market.

Changes in the selling power of suppliers

If a supplier has a dominant position in a market, it has greater freedom to choose prices and general conditions of sale. This situation applies in the global energy market, where the Russian government has substantial control over the sale of oil and gas to businesses in Western Europe. This allows the Russian government considerable freedom in pricing decisions but means that businesses in Western Europe that are reliant on this source of energy experience difficulty in controlling and forecasting costs of production. It has obvious implications for price competitiveness.

Suppliers with selling power may only be able to exercise such power in the short term, especially if they exploit it to charge what customers consider to be excessive prices. The reaction of customers in this situation will be to find alternative suppliers or, if this is not possible, to find substitute products or cut consumption of the relatively expensive good or service.

5.2 The responses of businesses to changes in the competitive environment

Businesses can respond in a variety of ways to changes in the competitive environment. Their responses will depend on the precise circumstances.

- **Takeovers or mergers.** A move towards a more oligopolistic market structure may result in smaller firms in that market joining together or buying one another, to give the new business sufficient scale to compete with larger rivals. Ironically, this will lead to an even more oligopolistic structure and may encourage further amalgamation. This process can be seen in a number of markets, such as banking in the UK.
- **Producing new products or cutting prices.** The arrival of new competitors or the creation of a dominant business may lead to existing producers increasing the range of products they offer or engaging in price cutting. At various times, British Airways has used both these techniques to compete with Ryanair and easyJet.
- **Seeking new markets.** Existing businesses could respond to new competitors or to dominant businesses by seeking to develop new markets where competition is less fierce. Some business airlines have moved to new routes when faced with direct competition from budget airlines. This might also be an appropriate strategy for a business that is facing a dominant customer.
- **Developing a different corporate strategy.** Increasing competition may lead to a business adopting a different strategy, such as becoming more innovative or moving to supply a different segment of the market — perhaps consumers seeking more exclusive products.
- **Seeking new suppliers or alternative types of supply.** As we saw earlier, customers may seek cheaper alternative supplies if a business charges what are considered to be excessive prices. Following the quadrupling of oil prices in the 1970s, many developed countries took action to reduce their dependence on oil. In 2008 the quantity of oil purchased by those countries is little higher than it was 30 years earlier, despite their economies have grown considerably over the intervening period. Governments, businesses and consumers have taken actions to reduce consumption of oil.

Examiner's tip

When responding to questions about changes in the competitive environment, you should consider the circumstances carefully. In developing your response, consider the strengths and weaknesses of the business, the resources available to it and the timescale over which it is able to respond.

Such advice is relevant whenever you are analysing and evaluating the responses of businesses to changes in the environments in which they operate.

CHAPTER 9 Managing change

Internal causes of change

What you need to know:

- the causes and effects of change in an organisation's size
- how new owners or leaders can cause change
- poor business performance as a catalyst for change

1.1 The causes and effects of change in an organisation's size

There are a number of reasons why an organisation might change its scale and thereby generate change within the organisation.

Mergers and takeovers

A **merger** is the combining of two or more firms into a single business following agreement by the firms' management teams and shareholders. A **takeover** occurs when one company acquires complete control of another by purchasing over 50% of its share capital. The types of merger and takeover are shown in Table 9.1.

Mergers	Takeovers
Mergers may be: • **Horizontal** – between firms at the same stage of production in the same market, offering economies of scale. • **Vertical** – between firms operating at different levels in the same market, providing certainty of supply or retail outlets. • **Conglomerate** – between firms in unrelated markets, reducing risk and allowing the transfer of good practice.	Takeovers can be horizontal, vertical or conglomerate. They can also be: • **Hostile** – where a predator company's attentions are unwelcome and the target may try to reject the move. The predator has only a limited time to persuade the target company's shareholders to accept the bid. • **Friendly** – where the company to be taken over welcomes the purchase and is likely to recommend that shareholders accept the bid.

Table 9.1 Types of merger and takeover

Merger activity tends to operate in cycles. However, the growing competitive pressure in a number of UK markets has forced many companies (particularly financial institutions) to merge in an attempt to increase efficiency by operating on a larger scale.

Businesses engage in mergers and takeovers for a number of reasons:

- **Growth.** Mergers and takeovers can be easy methods of expansion. However, it can be risky to spend large sums of capital on combining with another, perhaps relatively unknown, business.
- **Managers can often derive satisfaction and career enhancement** from increasing the scale of their organisation.
- If businesses have available liquid funds, purchasing other businesses can be profitable. Some businesses make enormous profits from **asset stripping** — buying businesses, breaking them up and selling off the profitable sections.
- A business may merge with or take over another company to achieve the benefits of **economies of scale**. This is most likely with horizontal mergers.
- Mergers and takeovers may be undertaken to **protect market share** by purchasing a rival that may prove a threat in years to come. Growth by this means also makes it more difficult and expensive for other companies to make a successful takeover bid.

In recent years, there have been a number of cases of companies splitting into two or more separate elements. Sometimes **demergers** follow a takeover that has not been successful, perhaps because the expected economies of scale have not materialised. Alternatively, companies may decide to sell off peripheral divisions to concentrate on their core activities.

Organic growth

Organic growth is a process of business expansion resulting from increased production, sales or both, rather than mergers or takeovers. Organic growth represents the true growth rate for a business. It is a good indicator of how well the business's management has used its resources to expand the organisation's profits.

Organic growth can be created in a number of ways, such as:
- successful promotion of the business's products
- maximising value added
- introducing innovative products

A business may need to borrow heavily to finance organic growth, although some businesses such as McDonald's achieve this through the use of franchising.

Retrenchment

Retrenchment occurs when a business becomes smaller. In effect, this is negative organic growth. There are a number of possible causes of retrenchment:
- changes in tastes and fashions
- technological developments making products obsolete
- the closure of subsidiary businesses

Examiner's tip

In the case of each of these causes of change, you should think about the effects on the organisation. Key issues might include levels of employment, product range and corporate image.

1.2 How new owners or leaders can cause change

It is not unusual for a business to have new owners and this can be a spur to change. We saw above that a business might be taken over by another, larger organisation. On occasions, one large business might sell a subsidiary business to another large organisation. For example, in March 2008 the Indian car manufacturer Tata purchased the Jaguar company from Ford for a reported £1,115 million.

The consequences of a new owner will depend to some extent on why the business has changed ownership. If the new owner was seeking an established and valued brand (as may be true in the case of Tata), the extent of change resulting might be relatively slight. In these circumstances, the new owner would want to maintain the image and product range. However, a new owner might have purchased a business because of the possibilities of improving its performance and generating higher profits. This could lead to substantial changes within the business, including job losses, the introduction of new products or entry into new markets.

Management buyouts

The new owners of a business may come from within. If a business (or part of it) is bought by the existing management team, this is known as a **management buyout**. The value of management buyouts has increased steadily since the middle of the 1990s.

Management buyouts may take place when:
- a company, or part of it, has underperformed over a period of time, but the management team considers that, perhaps with more finance, profits could be generated
- a family-owned (and possibly benevolent) business decides to sell out, but does so to the existing management team in the hope of maintaining employment and a traditional manner of production

The advantages of management buyouts are set out below.
- For the seller there is a benefit in selling what may be a loss-making activity.
- A successful buyout may lead to the business's flotation on the Stock Exchange and great wealth for the management team.
- The buyers have the challenge and enjoyment of running their own business.
- A management buyout may result in jobs being saved, as the alternative might have been closure.

The disadvantages are as follows:
- Many management buyouts fail within a few years because the business is fundamentally unprofitable.
- Management buyouts are often accompanied by rationalisation and job losses as the firm attempts to improve financial performance.
- Management buyouts frequently have limited access to capital and this can hinder their performance.

1.3 Poor business performance as a catalyst for change

A business may perform badly in a number of ways. It can lose market share, allow its product range to become outdated or suffer from a decline in its corporate image. However, the performance of most private sector businesses is judged most effectively by financial measures. Thus, a business suffering from declining profits or a substantial reduction in its share price may be purchased by another business.

A decline in profitability is often the catalyst for change in companies. Shareholders can be expected to be unhappy in such circumstances, as their dividends may be cut, or no dividends may be paid. This can be accompanied by falling share prices, resulting in shareholders losing money. This scenario is likely to provoke calls for change, and directors may be voted out of office by angry shareholders.

The other key cause of poor business performance which acts as a catalyst for change is a lack of cash flow. If a severe shortage of cash occurs, this can lead to a company becoming insolvent, in which case it is legally obliged to cease trading. In such a situation, a business is vulnerable to takeover. In any event, a shortage of cash often results in dramatic changes within an organisation.

2 *Planning for change*

What you need to know:
- the purpose of corporate plans
- internal and external influences on corporate plans
- the value of corporate plans

2.1 The purpose of corporate plans

Corporate plans

A **corporate (or strategic) plan** is a long-term strategy by which a business hopes to achieve its corporate objectives. This type of planning involves matching the corporate objectives to the resources available. The corporate plan is therefore the strategic process of allocating resources within an organisation in order to achieve its strategic or corporate aims.

From the corporate plan, the plans for all the different functions of the business (e.g. marketing, finance, HR and operations) can be derived. Once the corporate plan has been decided, each section of the business can plan how it will contribute to the overall strategy.

The purpose of corporate plans is to make sure that managers are looking ahead and thinking about what they want to achieve and how to achieve it, rather than just drifting along. Producing the plan is also a useful exercise because it forces managers to consider the organisation's strengths and weaknesses in relation to its environment, and to think about the how all the different elements of the firm interrelate.

Corporate plans also have an important function of ensuring that the separate departments (marketing, finance, HR and operations) are working together in pursuit of the business's overall or corporate objectives. The corporate plan pulls together the functional plans and provides a sense of common purpose.

Contingency planning

All plans, and especially long-term ones, can go wrong. Businesses should prepare for this and also for the unexpected. A business may put a **contingency plan** into operation in the following circumstances:
- **During a sudden slump in demand.** This was experienced by many car manufacturers following the global financial crisis in 2008, when UK sales of new cars fell by over 20%.
- **When a business becomes the object of the attentions of a pressure group.** For example, Monsanto was subject to much criticism following its involvement in the development of genetically modified crops. The company attracted a great deal of adverse publicity before announcing a major change of strategy.
- **When a new and highly efficient competitor emerges.** For example, British Airways sales have suffered as a result of the emergence of easyJet and Ryanair as rivals.

Contingency plans should contain a number of common elements:
- an identified team headed by an experienced manager to assume control in the event of a crisis
- sufficient resources to deal with the problem — the crisis team will need financial resources, communications technology and access to experts in order to cope with the unexpected

- effective communications systems that can identify the nature and causes of the problem as well as prepare appropriate responses
- efficient links with the media, as ill-informed speculation can be damaging to the organisation

Contingency plans need to be reviewed regularly to ensure that they are relevant and up to date. It may be necessary to test the effectiveness of contingency plans and systems by simulating a crisis and practising the planned response.

2.2 Internal and external influences on corporate plans

A number of internal and external factors may influence senior managers in constructing their corporate or strategic plans.

Internal factors

Internal factors include.

- **The organisation's mission statement and corporate objectives.** If, for example, these make reference to becoming market leader, the associated corporate plan will probably address issues such as quality, customer service and, perhaps, takeovers.
- **The resources available to the business.** Grand plans for expansion may founder if a business has access to only relatively small amounts of finance. Similarly, improving customer service may require greater (and more highly skilled) human resources than those available to the business at present. Strategies are normally based on a business's strengths.

External factors

Factors outside the organisation are likely to have a substantial impact on the contents of its corporate plan.

- **The actions of competitors.** Managers set corporate objectives and plan their associated strategies to achieve these objectives with the aim of operating in profitable markets. Actions of competitors (e.g. a competitor bringing out a new and revolutionary product) can affect the profitability of markets and in turn have knock-on effects on corporate objectives.
- **The state of the market and the economy.** A growing market is likely to result in more expansive corporate plans, not least because the business will probably have access to greater quantities of resources, not least funding. A recession, as experienced by many countries during and after 2008, will result in more conservative corporate plans, perhaps looking to protect the business's market position during troubled times.

It is normal for corporate plans to be determined and operated by senior managers within the business. However, some business analysts (e.g. Tom Peters) have argued that autonomous workgroups should contribute to the generation of corporate plans. Over recent years, large companies, such as British Airways, have introduced staff training with the aim of reinforcing company values and encouraging all staff to contribute to the achievement of corporate objectives.

The internal and external influences on corporate plans are summarised in Figure 9.1 overleaf.

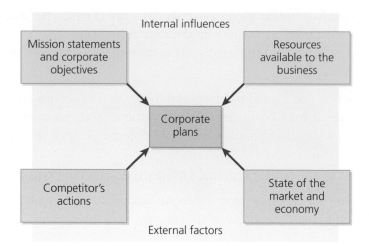

Figure 9.1 Internal and external influences on corporate plans

---

Examiner's tip

The specification requires you to evaluate the importance of influences on corporate plans such as those set out here. You should be prepared to make and justify judgements about the key influences on a business's corporate plans. Think about whether external or internal influences are more dominant and make sure that you understand the company's financial position and its market standing.

2.3 The value of corporate plans

A corporate plan offers two major advantages to a business. First, the process of corporate planning requires senior managers in an organisation to look forward and to consider where they want the organisation to be and how it should achieve these objectives. This process can encourage managers to consider the strengths and weaknesses of the business and how these can be used to respond to threats and to take advantages of any opportunities that may exist. This process should help to develop a more proactive (as opposed to a reactive) style of management. This can help businesses to become innovative and market leaders.

A second benefit is coordination. In large businesses, possibly trading in many markets across several countries, a corporate plan sets out the business's strategy and this can guide all managers in drawing up their plans. In this way, the sometimes disparate elements of the organisation can work together to achieve common goals.

But there are dangers in slavishly following a corporate plan, especially in a changing environment. The effects of the global financial crisis in 2008 will have prompted many businesses to amend their corporate plans, perhaps to adopt more defensive positions. Following a plan, irrespective of changing factors, can result in managers taking incorrect decisions. An effective corporate plan should be a work in progress.

3 *Key influences on the change process: leadership*

What you need to know:
- the meaning of leadership
- the range of leadership styles
- internal and external influences on leadership styles
- the role of leadership in managing change
- the importance of leadership

3.1 The meaning of leadership

A leader is a person who rules, guides or inspires others. Leaders have authority that has been delegated to them by the organisation. Acceptance of a leader's power by the staff can result from a number of factors:

- **Tradition.** In many long-established firms, senior management posts are handed down from generation to generation in the same family. Members of the next generation of owners are accepted in senior positions, irrespective of their ability to do the job.
- **The way a person was appointed.** If the process of selection is seen to be fair, the outcome will be generally supported.
- **Personality.** Some leaders derive their authority from charisma and lead others purely by the strength of their personality. Such leaders can develop tremendous loyalty among their staff.

A good leader has a number of qualities. Although the precise list might be debatable, the necessary qualities may include:

- a positive self-image and associated self-confidence
- being informed and knowledgeable
- having the ability to think creatively and innovatively
- having the ability to act quickly and decisively
- possessing an air of authority
- having first-class communication skills (including listening)
- being able to solve problems, often under pressure

A leader differs from a manager. A manager sets objectives and seeks the most efficient use of resources. A leader motivates people and brings the best out of individuals in pursuit of agreed objectives.

3.2 The range of leadership styles

Some writers on leadership have argued that leaders are born. This is known as **trait theory**. Such analysts attempt to identify the features of personality that one would expect to find in a good leader, as in the list above.

Others have rejected this view and contend that people can be taught to be good leaders. This school of thought gives a central role to **training** in successful leadership.

In spite of the above dispute, four basic categories of leadership style are used widely for purposes of analysis. These are **democratic**, **paternalistic**, **authoritarian** and **laissez-faire**. Each style has advantages and disadvantages, and each is perhaps appropriate in particular circumstances (see Table 9.2).

Type/features	Democratic	Paternalistic	Authoritarian	Laissez-faire
Description	Democratic leadership entails running a business on the basis of decisions agreed by the majority.	The paternalistic approach is dictatorial, but decisions are intended to be in the best interests of the employees.	An authoritarian leadership style keeps information and decision making among the senior managers.	Laissez-faire leadership means the leader has a peripheral role, leaving staff to manage the business.
Key features	Encourages participation and makes use of delegation.	Leader explains decisions and ensures social and leisure needs are met.	Sets objectives and allocates tasks. Leader retains control throughout.	Leader evades duties of management and uncoordinated delegation occurs.
Communication	Extensive, two-way. Encourages contributions from subordinates.	Generally downwards, though feedback will take place.	One-way communication, downwards from leader to subordinate.	Mainly horizontal communication, though little communication occurs.
Uses	When complex decisions are made requiring a range of specialist skills.	Can appear democratic, but is really 'soft' autocracy.	Useful when quick decisions are required.	Can encourage production of highly creative work by subordinates.
Advantages	Commitment to business, satisfaction and quality of work may all improve.	Can engender loyalty, and frequently enjoys low labour turnover due to emphasis on social needs.	Decisions and direction of business will be consistent. May project image of confident, well-managed business.	May bring the best out of highly professional or creative groups.
Disadvantages	Slow decision making and need for consensus may avoid taking 'best' decisions.	Really autocratic and can result in groups becoming highly dependent. They may become dissatisfied with leader.	Lack of information, so subordinates highly dependent on leaders; supervision needed	May not be deliberate, but bad management — staff lack focus and sense of direction. Much dissatisfaction.

Table 9.2 Leadership styles

Examiner's tip

Democratic leadership is not always the best style. It is important to relate the style of leadership to the circumstances. The factors below would influence the style of management selected.

3.3 Internal and external influences on leadership styles

Leadership styles may vary according to the circumstances. The appropriate method will depend on the personality of the leader, the ability and skills of the workforce and the timescale. There are also a number of internal and external factors which may influence the leadership style adopted in any circumstances.

- **The culture of the business.** If employees are used to autocratic management, preparation and (especially) training will be required before a change of style.
- **The nature of the task.** For example, a complex and lengthy task is more likely to need democratic management; if it requires a laissez-faire approach, a laissez-faire leadership style may be more appropriate.
- **The nature of the workforce.** Less skilled and large groups of employees might be more likely to respond to autocratic styles of management. The personalities and potential of the workforce will also influence the style of leadership adopted.
- **The personality and skills of the leader.** Good communication and other interpersonal skills might encourage democratic leadership. Alternatively, high levels of knowledge of the task may encourage a more autocratic approach.
- **Takeovers and mergers.** If a business is taken over by or merges with another organisation, the leadership style may change to reflect the changed ownership of the organisation. A business taking over another may impose its own management team and leadership style.

Tannenbaum and Schmidt developed this idea further. They argued that the style of leadership depends on the prevailing circumstances. Leaders should have the ability to exercise a range of leadership styles and should deploy them as appropriate. Therefore, a good leader is one who has the talent to adapt his or her style to the circumstances. Table 9.3 illustrates the range or continuum of styles a leader might use.

Use of authority by the leader					
				Degree of freedom enjoyed by subordinates	
Tells	**Sells**	**Tests**	**Consults**	**Joins**	**Delegates**
Leader	*Leader*	*Leader*	*Leader*	*Leader*	*Leader*
Owns and resolves total problem and instructs subordinates.	Resolves problem and informs subordinates.	Tackles problem but seeks opinions.	Proposes alternatives and seeks recommendations.	Works with subordinates in taking decisions.	Passes authority to subordinates for decision making.
Subordinate	*Subordinate*	*Subordinate*	*Subordinate*	*Subordinate*	*Subordinate*
Simply responds.	Receives explanation and acts.	Expresses views on decision.	Discusses alternatives and gives recommendations.	Helps shape objectives and solutions. Views accepted.	Exercises authority and owns the decisions taken.

Table 9.3 Tannenbaum and Schmidt's continuum of leadership behaviour

One of the dilemmas faced by leaders is the tension between the needs of people and the needs of the task. Some of the facets of democratic leadership, such as two-way communication, may be difficult to enact in circumstances in which a task has to be completed in a short time. On the other hand, leaders who focus on the task may damage the morale of colleagues and the efficiency of the organisation by not involving colleagues. This dilemma reinforces the view that there is no single 'best' style of leadership and that approaches appropriate to the circumstances should be adopted.

3.4 The role of leadership in managing change

Leadership can influence the process of change profoundly in a number of ways:

- **Setting objectives.** Leaders establish the goals that the change process is intended to achieve. By setting realistic, appropriate but challenging goals, the leader can set the tone of the entire process and provide it with a sense of purpose and direction.
- **Appointing or being the change project 'champion'.** We will consider this more fully on pages 134–37, but the leader can be a role model for change and espouse its cause at every opportunity.
- **Making sufficient resources available at the right time.** This is an essential element of a successful change programme. A leader will have ultimate control of financial, human and other resources, and by making them available at the right time, he or she can lubricate the wheels of change. For example, a business planning to extend its product range may need large sums of finance at an early stage in the process to pay staff salaries and for research and development.
- **Ensuring that the other parts of the business support change.** A change programme may have a negative impact on some elements of the business. Some managers may feel that the development damages their prestige or position in the organisation. It is a key role for leaders to ensure that everyone supports the project and does not take steps to prevent its success.
- **Using available talent as fully as possible.** Change can be a pressured and stressful time for an organisation. A good leader will seek to make use of all the talents that are available within the organisation to manage it as effectively as possible. The leader may also recognise the need to bring in external expertise (even at considerable cost) to manage change projects.

Leadership is not the only factor that determines whether change is managed successfully. Section 6 of this chapter looks in more detail at this matter.

3.5 The importance of leadership

Does it really matter to a business whether it has highly skilled and conscientious leaders? As in so many cases, the answer to this will depend on the circumstances, as shown in Table 9.4.

In spite of this distinction, it is probably true to say that good leadership is important in the long term for any business. Even a business with a strong market share, high profits and well-established brands may find its position declining unless appropriate decisions and actions are taken. Rivals may develop new, more sophisticated products that are highly valued by consumers. Sales and profits may diminish and the firm's position in the market may decline. A business (or a leader, for that matter) should not take success for granted.

When good leadership would be really important	When good leadership may be desirable, but not so critical
• In a highly competitive market, where profit margins are slim. • In the early stages of a business's life, when it is attempting to establish itself. • At a time of particularly rapid and substantial change. • At a time of crisis — for example, when consumers lose confidence in a product, or a takeover is threatened.	• When a business is well established with strong brands and high levels of consumer loyalty. • In a market where patterns of demand change infrequently. • Where the workforce is highly skilled and motivated — the role of a leader might be more administrative in these circumstances.

Table 9.4 The importance of leadership

4 *Key influences on the change process: culture*

What you need to know:
• types of organisational culture
• reasons for, and problems in, changing organisational culture
• the importance of organisational culture

4.1 Types of organisational culture

An organisation's **culture** is the attitudes, ideas and beliefs that are shared by its employees. An organisation's culture is neither static nor permanent. It develops over time in response to many factors.

Various different types of organisational culture exist. A number of writers have provided frameworks for classifying cultures. The list below is based on the writing of Charles Handy.

• **Traditional or role culture.** Businesses with this type of culture are conventional, operate in a bureaucratic manner and value conventional behaviour. Employees are expected to follow the rules and emphasis is given to hierarchy and roles within the organisation.
• **Person-orientated culture.** This focuses on fulfilling the needs of individuals within an organisation. It allows individuals freedom to shape their jobs and operate with a degree of independence.
• **Task culture.** This focuses on solving problems. Expert teams or groups are assembled to tackle particular problems or to complete projects. This culture attaches importance to expertise, flexibility and creativity.
• **Power culture.** This places considerable emphasis on personal charisma and risk taking. It disregards procedures and values entrepreneurship.

In addition, a **change culture** can be highly valued in some circumstances. This refers to a flexible, responsive organisation that is capable of adapting effectively and quickly to external stimuli.

4.2 Reasons for, and problems in, changing organisational culture

Reasons for changing culture

Changing corporate cultures has attracted a great deal of attention in management circles over recent years. Some managers consider that their organisations have an inappropriate culture. For example, a business with a role culture, with closely defined and highly specialised jobs, may find it difficult to operate in a fiercely competitive market that requires adaptability and a high degree of creativity from employees.

An organisation may seek to change its culture for a number of other reasons:
- It may be subject to a takeover bid or have agreed a merger with another business, and the organisation's existing culture conflicts with that of the other organisation.
- Changing locations may result in cultures being considered inappropriate. For example, a business relocating much of its operation overseas may consider that a traditional culture is less effective when people are in several distant locations. It may be that the business seeks to move towards a task culture in these circumstances.
- The appointment of a new chief executive may be the catalyst for changing a culture. If this is an external appointment and the new employee has been highly successful in an organisation with a different culture, he or she may decide to introduce the same culture to the business.
- Managers may consider that the present culture makes the business uncompetitive. For example, if rivals are more flexible and responsive to changing market conditions, the managers of a business may seek to move from a traditional to a task-orientated culture.

Problems in changing culture

If a culture is strongly embedded within the organisation, it may prove difficult to change. A number of factors determine how strong an organisation's culture may be:
- **The rate of labour turnover.** If a business experiences a low level of labour turnover, the prevailing culture is likely to be reinforced. It is much less likely that existing employees (and groups of employees) will change their culture. Change is easier to effect when large number of new employees enter the business regularly.
- **The nature and background of the workforce.** The culture of some groups of employees has been developed over a number of years (and perhaps in difficult and testing circumstances). In situations such as this, the culture may prove almost impossible to change. The culture of workers in many of the UK's former mining communities was strongly embedded, having evolved over a number of generations.
- **The extent to which the organisation's structure reinforces the culture.** A role culture may be difficult to change if emphasis is given to hierarchy and position. It may be necessary to change the structure to change the culture.
- **Informal communication.** If the operation of the business allows employees the opportunity to communicate informally — during regular tea breaks, for example — the existing culture is likely to be reinforced.

It is doubtful whether a business's culture can be changed significantly in the short term. A key factor may be the extent to which the factors determining the strength of the culture can be affected by management action. Changing an organisation's culture may require the business's structure to be reorganised, the hiring of new employees and perhaps new policies such as empowerment. It is not just the shop-floor employees who have to change, but also the management team; the existing culture may be firmly embedded here too.

It may also be a mistake to change one inappropriate culture for another that becomes equally inappropriate in a short space of time. This may happen to organisations that operate in a volatile environment. It may be optimal for managers to seek to inculcate a change culture that is flexible and responsive, and less likely to become unsuitable in the modern world of business.

4.3 The importance of organisational culture

It can be argued that a successful business focuses on the behaviour of employees. If employees have the right attitudes and behave in the desired manner, the business will flourish. Thus, managing the corporate culture is believed by many managers to be a vital element of commercial success.

To some extent this argument might be true. For most businesses and particularly those in a changing environment, developing the appropriate culture will be beneficial. It can also enhance the competitiveness of an organisation. Having an appropriate culture may limit conflict and lessen the possibility of industrial disputes. It may (in the long term) reduce labour turnover and improve employee motivation, once resistance to the change in culture has been overcome. Changing the culture of an organisation can make the business more innovative, encouraging the development of new, modern products. All of these factors should help a business to improve its competitive performance.

However, other factors are important determinants of a business's competitiveness, such as exchange rates, interest rates and government economic policies. Similarly, the actions of competitors (e.g. introducing new, advanced products) will affect the competitiveness of firms. Finally, the public's perception of the business (perhaps shaped by the actions of pressure groups) will also play a role in determining competitiveness.

Any judgement on the importance of culture in determining a business's competitiveness has to recognise that many important factors are beyond the control of the management team. While changing culture may improve the internal performance of a business, the environment in which it operates may have an adverse impact on the organisation's competitiveness. Culture can, however, determine how effectively the business responds to external change and can be argued to be a key long-term determinant of competitiveness.

5 *Making strategic decisions*

What you need to know:
- the significance of information management
- the value of different approaches to decision making
- influences on corporate decision making

5.1 The significance of information management

Information management is the collection and management of information from one or more sources in the organisation, and the distribution of that information to the relevant employees.

Businesses might need to manage a range of information, including:
- data relating to costs of production and other financial aspects of the business
- marketing information relating to sales, market growth, competitors' actions and changes in consumer tastes

- operations data, such as capacity utilisation, availability of resources used in production and quality performance data
- HR data on labour turnover, wage costs, productivity and so on

Most of the information on this list is numerical in form. However, businesses also need qualitative data which, for example, explain customers' attitudes to the business and its brands or products.

Businesses need to collect the right information, to collate and analyse it, and to make it available to the right people in an organisation. Information helps managers to make decisions at all levels within the organisation.

- **Strategic decisions.** Information is perhaps most necessary before such long-term and important decisions are taken. The process of planning is highly dependent on having the right information to hand. For example, information on relevant costs in different countries will help to determine operational elements of the corporate plan, such as where to locate a new production facility.
- **Marketing and other functional decisions.** A business will need up-to-date and accurate information on costs, recent sales, competitors' actions and, most importantly, consumers' needs if it is to supply the market with the right products at the right place and at the right price. Many managers would not take marketing decisions without a range of relevant information.
- **Tactical decisions.** Even for a relatively simple decision, such as whether to increase production of a product over the next few days, relevant information is essential. Managers will need information on the actual level of orders, the staff that are available and stocks of other resources used in the production process.

A well-managed business will manage its information efficiently. This means that it is available promptly to the people who need it, is up to date and is in a form that can be readily understood.

5.2 The value of different approaches to decision making

It is entirely possible for managers to make even the most important decisions on the basis of a hunch or intuition. This might lead a manager to take a decision that is not supported by the data that are available, or which is not a standard or expected decision in the circumstances. Some managers believe that really great decisions are made by hunches.

However, other managers take a more scientific approach to decision making. A number of models or theories can be used.

Examiner's tip

The models listed below are not the only ones that you can use to answer questions on this part of the specification. Questions will not require you to write about any particular model of decision making. Rather, you will be able to select your own.

Ansoff's matrix

We first encountered this model in Chapter 3 in connection with decisions on marketing strategy. You will remember that it represents a useful framework for considering the relationship between marketing and overall strategy. The technique considers product

and market growth and analyses the degree of risk attached to the range of options open to the business. Key findings of Ansoff's matrix are:

● Staying with what you know (e.g. market penetration) represents relatively little risk.
● Moving into new markets with new products is a high-risk strategy.

Assessment is made of the value of each option.

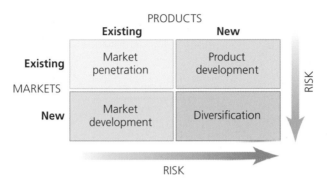

Figure 9.2 Ansoff's matrix

Decision trees

Strategic management is made easier by reducing uncertainty in decision making. Alternatively, senior managers might seek to measure the degree of uncertainty involved in a decision and take it into account. Uncertainty can be measured by probability, and the calculation of probability can be used to assess the extent of uncertainty in any decision.

Central to the use of decision trees is the calculation of the expected value of each aspect of a particular decision. Businesses can calculate the expected value of an outcome by multiplying the probability of that outcome by the benefit that the business can expect if it happens.

Example

A business is considering whether or not to launch a new product. If it does so and the product succeeds, the business forecasts £1.6 million profits. The product has a 0.25 (25%) probability of success. The expected value from the new product will be:

£1.6 million × 0.25 = £400,000

Decision trees can be used to represent and offer some evaluation of the choices open to a business. There are various stages in constructing a decision tree:

(1) Identify the courses of action available to the business.

(2) Assess the likely outcomes of each of these actions.

(3) Attach probabilities to each action available to the firm.

(4) Estimate the likely financial returns from each action.

(5) Calculate the expected value of each action.

(6) Choose the course of action generating the highest expected value.

In decision trees, as shown in Figure 9.3:
- A decision point is indicated by a square.
- Circles represent alternatives with probabilities attached.
- The probabilities of each event taking place are shown by decimal figures on the appropriate line.
- Any costs associated with decisions are shown next to the decision and preceded by a minus sign.
- The benefits of outcomes are listed on the right-hand side of the decision tree.

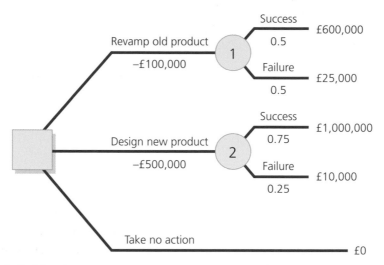

Figure 9.3 A decision tree

The outcomes for the choices available to the business in Figure 9.3 are as follows:

Revamp old product = (0.5 × £600,000) + (0.5 × £25,000) – £100,000 = £212,500

Design new product = (0.75 × £1,000,000) + (0.25 × £10,000) – £500,000 = £252,500

Do nothing = £0

Given the anticipated probabilities and the forecast revenues and costs, a logical choice in these circumstances would be to design a new product.

The advantages of using decision trees are as follows:
- They encourage a logical approach to decision making by businesses and consideration of all possibilities.
- They are especially useful in circumstances where accurate values can be attached to options.
- They help businesses to take risk into account when taking decisions.
- They discourage instinctive decisions or use of 'gut reactions'.

They have the following disadvantages:
- It is difficult to get accurate data, especially relating to probabilities.
- Management bias can be introduced into the data to achieve a desired decision.
- Change (particularly in the business environment) may affect the accuracy of the decision.

Porter's strategic matrix

Michael Porter of the Harvard Business School is one of the foremost business writers in the world today. One of his best-known contributions to management thinking is his strategic matrix (Figure 9.4). Its purpose is to assist managers in assessing strategy. It assesses whether the business is aiming at producing low-cost or differentiated products. Simultaneously, it judges whether the business is operating in a niche or a mass market.

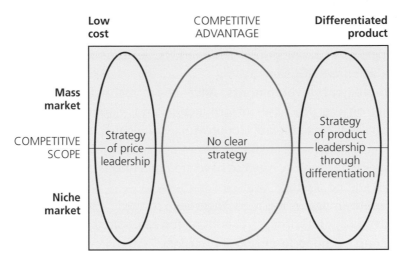

Figure 9.4 Porter's strategic matrix

The fundamental point of Porter's theory is that, whether operating in a niche or a mass market, a business should aim either to be a low-cost producer or to sell a product that is highly differentiated from those of rivals. It should not allow its strategy to drift towards the middle of the matrix, seeking neither price nor product leadership.

A number of airlines have pursued very successful strategies based on price leadership. Arguably the most successful has been Ryanair. At the same time, British Airways has not always operated a clear strategy, which may, in part, explain some of the problems that the company has encountered over recent years.

Examiner's tip

Many questions focus on business strategy. Using a model such as one of the above to analyse the strengths and weaknesses of a decision can assist you in justifying any judgement you make about its appropriateness.

5.3 Influences on corporate decision making

There are a number of factors that can influence the process of corporate decision making. Some of these are set out below.
- **The business's history.** The business's strategic decisions will be shaped by its history to a greater or lesser extent. If, for example, a business has a history of supplying unusual and innovative products, and has gained a competitive advantage from this, its senior managers will take this into account when making important decisions.
- **Competitors' decisions.** It is possible that a business's strategic decisions will have to mirror, or respond in some way to, those taken by its competitors. Thus, if a business's rivals relocate to eastern Europe to reduce manufacturing costs, the business in question is likely to make a strategic response to this, or risk losing price competitiveness. It may also relocate, employ more technology in its production

process in an attempt to reduce costs, or possibly look to reposition itself as a supplier of premium-quality products. This latter action would reduce the need for price competitiveness, or help to make demand for its product less price elastic.

- **The economic environment.** A positive economic environment (steady economic growth, low inflation, stable exchange rates, etc.) may encourage corporate planners and decisions-makers to take more risky decisions: for example, in developing new products or expanding into new markets. An economic downturn could result in more defensive decision making.
- **Technological developments.** Advances in technology can have a considerable impact on the processes of production and therefore may encourage strategic decision-makers to replace labour with technology or to decide to locate in countries with higher wage costs, but access to better support for technological production. Changes in technology can also have profound effects on the products that businesses supply and on strategic decisions in this area.
- **Corporate image.** A business might take strategic decisions intended to promote a positive corporate image. This may, for example, entail senior managers taking decisions intended to project the business as environmentally friendly. Marks and Spencer has recently taken a decision to project a greener image through its Plan A campaign.

Figure 9.5 Influences on corporate decision making

Examiner's tip

There are many possible decisions on a business's strategic planning. This section only considers a few of the possibilities. You should consider the scenario to which any examination question relates and seek to identify the most relevant ones, rather than simply relying on this list.

6   *Implementing and managing change*

What you need to know:
- techniques to implement and manage change successfully
- assessing factors that promote and resist change

6.1 Techniques to implement and manage change successfully

Using a project plan

A project plan for use in a change programme entails a number of stages:

Initiation stage

Writing a plan for a project provides the necessary framework for thinking about how it will deliver. The first stage of any project is therefore to define what change you are hoping to effect. There should be a clear business reason for undertaking the project and for why the work is important. The opening elements of the plan should state what the project needs to accomplish: that is, its aims and objectives.

Making a plan

The people writing the project plan need to decide the following issues:

- What are the strategies and methods to be used to achieve the change objectives?
- What will and will not be covered by the project plan? This is called the **scope and boundaries**.
- What factors are critical to the success of the project?
- Who is going to be involved in the project team and what are their strengths and areas of expertise?
- What budget is available for the plan?
- What are the project outcomes? These can be physical things (tangible deliverables), such as websites, reports and products; or intangible knowledge and experiences.

Work breakdown structure

Any project can be broken down into a set of simpler tasks, which when carried out in sequence will achieve the desired outcome. This process is given a rather grand name, **work breakdown structure**. If any task is too complicated to organise easily, it should be broken down into a series of smaller, less complex tasks. Managers can then provide clear instructions about what is to be done, and estimate the time and resources required.

Task allocation

The next stage is to decide who will be responsible for carrying out the individual tasks that have been identified. Task allocation also states when the tasks will be completed to ensure that they are carried out in the right sequence.

Executing the project

Once the project is under way, progress must be reviewed at regular intervals to ensure the project is still on track. Two major elements are used by managers to control their projects:

- **Milestones** — clear targets of what you will deliver by when (short-term goals). If these are not met, managers will need to take corrective action to put the project back on time.
- **Effective communication** — it is essential to have an early warning system for any problems to allow you to take corrective action. All team members should report back regularly on progress, and meetings may be arranged to facilitate this process.

Project evaluation

Evaluating the success of a project plan requires that a number of important questions are answered:

- Were objectives of the project met?
- Was the outcome of suitable quality, and did it meet the needs of the project's stakeholders?
- Was enough time allocated?
- Did everyone understand the project definition and their roles within it?
- What lessons did we learn from our mistakes and successes?

Establishing a project team

Putting together a project team can help a business to manage change successfully. A project team can have a range of different and complementary skills that can lead to greater levels of creativity, ingenuity and imagination. Together, the talents of team members are more likely to be successful, and they are also likely to provide a network of support and commitment to the aims of the project.

But developing a team is not a guarantee that the project will be completed successfully. Assembling the right *balance* of team members is essential. Managers responsible for recruiting team members need to think about the skills that the team requires and the range of tasks that have to be carried out to complete the project.

A successful team is likely to have a number of important characteristics:

- **It should be small and manageable.** Having between four and eight people is best. This will help the team to develop, should allow for a sufficient range of skills, but will lessen the chance of conflict.
- **The team's skills should be complementary.** It should have a range of technical, functional and professional skills appropriate to its task. Well-balanced teams contain people who can approach a task systematically, solve problems, decide on actions, and use appropriate techniques to carry them out. They need a good range of interpersonal skills, cohesion and a willingness to contribute to the team.
- **The team must have a common and agreed purpose.** Teams need clearly defined objectives and an agreed timescale. This common purpose will help to focus efforts and to reduce debates and conflict.
- **The team must have the authority to make decisions.** This has the potential to motivate the team, as it offers the opportunity to meet higher-level motivational needs.
- **The team must be accountable for results.** The team must be willing and able to take collective and individual responsibility for their objectives and results.
- **The team must have the necessary resources.** These resources may include staff and finance, as well as physical equipment and research systems on which to base decisions.
- **The team needs a leader.** He or she can help to keep a focus on the task and motivate team members towards the common goal. The leader needs the ability to assess the situation and manage in a number of styles to take the project forward.

Project champions

A **project champion** is a person who has the role of supporting and driving forward a particular project. He or she can play a vital role in managing change projects. Their job is to drive a project forward, advocating its benefits, assisting the team and helping to navigate any problems to keep the project on track.

A good project champion will possess a number of personal characteristics. They will be focused on achievement and completing the project within the agreed timescale and within budget. They could be described as a proactive 'doer'. Project champions generally have positive attitudes and are able to motivate other members of the team, as well as being able to generate enthusiasm and cooperation. Sebastian Coe could be described as a project champion for the London Olympics.

6.2 Assessing factors that promote and resist change

There are a number of factors that can lead to change being resisted:

- **Unclear or unrealistic objectives.** These can result in employees who are implementing change lacking a clear sense of direction and being unable to judge their progress.
- **Uncommitted staff and/or managers.** A time of change is one where employees are often expected to work harder, to work on unfamiliar tasks and to put in additional hours. In such circumstances, any lack of commitment can be serious.
- **Failure to assess risks.** Risk is the chance of something going wrong. There are a number of factors that represent risk in relation to change projects. Delays can occur which threaten the timely completion of the project. If managers have not allowed for this or have not prepared contingency plans, the success of the entire project may be threatened. Other sources of risk that must be planned for are overspending and the loss of key employees (perhaps due to illness or moving to a new job) at some stage during the project.

However, there are a number of things that managers of change projects can do to increase the chances of a project succeeding:

- **Give it sufficient resources.** This may refer to money, but equally important will be staffing and providing people with the right skills. Thus, if a change project involves entering a new market overseas, including people with appropriate language skills as part of the project team will be essential.
- **Provide training where necessary.** Managers should not assume that members of project teams have all the necessary skills to complete the tasks involved. A programme of training may be required before the project plan can be implemented.
- **Allow a realistic timescale.** Project teams should not be placed under too much time pressure to complete the tasks. This can result in poor-quality work and demotivation, and may, in the worst cases, lead to the failure of the project.

1 *General advice in preparing for Unit 4*

1.1 The examination

Key facts relating to this examination are set out below:

- Duration: 1 hour and 45 minutes.
- A two-part examination.
- Section A comprises two questions based on research tasks you will have completed earlier. You must choose *one* of these.
- Section B is one essay from a choice of three.
- Total marks available: 80.
- Available: January and June from January 2010.

This unit is **synoptic** — this means that it pulls together all the material from the entire AS and A2 specification. Although questions are based on the Unit 4 specification, you can draw on material from other elements of the specification to support your answers.

Performing well on this final paper will be essential for anyone who is aiming to achieve an A* grade for the whole A-level qualification.

A copy of AQA's specimen Unit 4 paper and marking scheme can be found at:

www.aqa.org.uk/qual/gce/pdf/business_studies_new.php

1.2 How to prepare for the Unit 4 examination

The advice offered earlier in Chapter 6 on preparing for the Unit 3 examination also applies in this case. You might benefit from looking back at pages 74–76

If you are unsure about the nature of application, analysis or evaluation, you should re-read the relevant parts of Chapter 6. As Table 10.1 shows, these skills carry 80% of the marks on this paper.

Skill	Marks	%
Knowledge	16	20
Application	16	20
Analysis	20	25
Evaluation	28	35
Total	80	100

Table 10.1 Mark allocations for Unit 4

There are two key additional elements of preparation for this paper:

- **Complete the research task.** The title of this task will be available from late January in your A2 year of study. It will require you to investigate in detail a small part of the Unit 4 specification. The research brief will give you precise guidance on the tasks to complete. Don't make too much of this task and extend your research beyond what is asked. Do, however, relate your research to a variety of large businesses producing goods and services and operating in different markets.

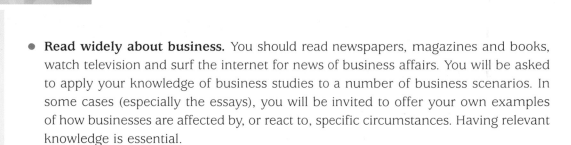
● **Read widely about business.** You should read newspapers, magazines and books, watch television and surf the internet for news of business affairs. You will be asked to apply your knowledge of business studies to a number of business scenarios. In some cases (especially the essays), you will be invited to offer your own examples of how businesses are affected by, or react to, specific circumstances. Having relevant knowledge is essential.

2   *A sample Unit 4 examination paper*

Section A: The research activity

It is not appropriate to write questions for a possible research task, since these will depend on the topic selected and the precise research guidance that is offered. You should, however, look at the specimen paper on the AQA website.

Section B: Essays

You should select one essay from those listed below.

1 To what extent should Marks and Spencer (or any other business with which you are familiar) regard the state of the UK economy as a threat or an opportunity?   **(40 marks)**

2 Discuss the ways in which a large multinational business might respond to the changing social environment in the UK.   **(40 marks)**

3 With reference to a business with which you are familiar, assess the importance of leadership in enabling the business to meet its objectives.   **(40 marks)**